ME
MYSELF
& WHY

ME
MYSELF
& WHY

DISCOVERING & LIVING YOUR VALUES

CHARITY BRADSHAW

ME, MYSELF & WHY
DISCOVERING & LIVING YOUR VALUES

© 2015 Charity Bradshaw.

Printed in the USA

ISBN (Print Version): 978-0-9962464-0-8

ISBN (Kindle Version): 978-0-9962464-1-5

ISBN (PDF eBook): 978-0-9962464-2-2

Library of Congress Control Number: 2015904839

All Rights Reserved. This book is protected by the copyright laws of the United States of America. This book may not be copied or reprinted for commercial gain or profit. The use of short quotations is permitted. Permission will be granted upon request. The author guarantees all contents are original and do not infringe upon the legal rights of any other person or work.

DISCLAIMER:

The opinions and recollections expressed in *Me, Myself & Why* are purely those of the author and may or may not reflect the opinions and recollections of others portrayed in the work.

This book has been prepared for publication by Wendy K. Walters and Palm Tree Publications, a division of Palm Tree Productions.

www.palmtreeproductions.com | www.wendykwalters.com

TO CONTACT THE AUTHOR:
WWW.CHARITYBRADSHAW.COM

DEDICATION

This book is dedicated to Luke, Kate, Natalie, my Angel baby, and Presley. Thank you for teaching me so much about life and love. I hope that this book and any that follow allow you to forever hear my heart.

THANKS ...

TED—

Thank you for loving me, for embracing and nurturing my boldness, for encouraging my creativity, for believing in me before I did and for giving me our wonderful children. Thank you for continuing to write the story of us with me.

MOM—

First of all, without your prompting there would be no book so for that we all say, "THANK YOU!" You saw this long before I ever could. Thank you for ALL you have done including birthing me, giving me sisters, prioritizing my education, surviving heartbreak, demonstrating how to honor your parents, giving me platforms to grow my confidence, building a legacy for our entire family and through it all, loving me so well.

SISTERS—

Thank you for everything. You all are amazing, successful, beautiful, smart and forgiving. Thank you for continuing to believe and invest in our family as a whole. Thank you for being lifetime hair and makeup experimentation models, for making me laugh till I cry, for doing puzzles, for spoiling my kids, and for being so generous. #barkerbeautiesforlife

WENDY—

Thank you for all you have invested into this project. You are a catalyst that when added to the mix, ideas are transformed into manuscripts and the ordinary into the extraordinary.

CONTENTS

- 11   **FOREWORD**
  BY JOAN HUNTER

- 13   **PREFACE**

- 17   CHAPTER 1
  525,600 MINUTES

- 35   CHAPTER 2
  O.P.V. OTHER PEOPLE'S VALUES

- 55   CHAPTER 3
  THE BEST POLICY

- 65   CHAPTER 4
  THE NEED FOR CONNECTION

- 87   CHAPTER 5
  OFFICE SPACE

- 103   CHAPTER 6
  CENTERED SELF

- 115   CHAPTER 7
  UNCOMMON CENTS

- 127   CHAPTER 8
  THE FAITH FILTER

- 141   CHAPTER 9
  CONCLUSION

- 153   MEET THE AUTHOR
  CHARITY BRADSHAW

* * * * * *

The longer you continue the behavior or pattern that came from someone or something else hurting you or disappointing you, the more power you give it and the less value you give you.

Discovering and living your value order provides you with freedom.

* * * * * *

FOREWORD
BY JOAN HUNTER

Writing a foreword for someone is a unique honor. It generally means you hold special value to the author in some way and they desire you to add the weight of your experience, expertise, wisdom, and influence to their work. Writing a foreword for your child is an honor that is difficult to describe.

When I was a young girl, I wanted a daughter named Charity. I was so excited when I gave birth to a little girl who had been born in my heart many years earlier, and now she was in my arms! From the moment I held her, I knew she was special. I felt God's joy over her and was astounded that He would trust me as a mother and allow me to watch over her as she grew. Now Charity is a wife and mother with four children of her own. As I watch her take care of them—teach them, love on them, cook for them ... I am extremely blessed and proud of her.

Charity is willing to fight for the things she holds dear and I appreciate this about her. She knows what she believes and is not easily swayed from any course where she has committed herself. In 2014 God spoke to Charity and her husband, Ted, that the time had come for them to pull up their roots and relocate from Nashville, Tennessee to Texas. Charity owned and operated a successful small business, Ted had a great job, they were active in an amazing church, and they had created a beautiful home there together. Moving was a leap of faith and I admire their courage to step out in obedience and follow God's voice.

This book is Charity's heart on a plate. She has opened herself up and shared what makes her tick, what makes her think the way she does, and what motivates her to make the choices she makes. She asks really great questions and gives you the opportunity to ask those same questions of yourself.

Her style is totally different than mine. The language she uses is her own, filtered through her experiences and colored by her humor and personality. She is called to reach out to a generation that has been turned off by "religion" and is in desperate need of a relationship with Jesus Christ.

It is my privilege to introduce *Me, Myself and Why*. This is Charity's first book and I know there are many more to come. I can't begin to express how proud I am of her for following God and pursuing the completion of this book. I celebrate her for giving up all that was comfortable and familiar in order to embrace what God has destined for her, blessed her with through our family line, and called her to do as only she can. My prayer is that as you read these pages, you will be challenged to define your own value order and choose your path in the light of His love.

Joan Hunter ♥
Author, Speaker, Evangelist

PREFACE

Some of my favorite times are when my husband and I stay up late and discuss our life strategies and make plans. We follow rabbit trails and play out scenarios trying to forecast the domino effect of different decisions. I began to realize that big changes result from little changes set in motion by small decisions. These small decisions seem benign and inconsequential, but can have as much impact on the direction of your life as the rudder of a ship. A two or three degree shift in one's heading doesn't change much in the beginning, but the further you follow that course, the greater the distance between where you were going and where you are. It is in these decisions—whether made intentionally or passively—that our destination is determined, our destiny.

Destiny is not a specific place and time, but rather a trajectory. It can evolve and change with the subtle or dramatic shifting of the helm, just like a ship. The journey of life is similar to a ship's voyage. The sooner you know where you want to go, the more time you have to get there with the best chances of succeeding.

- How do you decide where you want to go?
- What helps you make your decisions?
- What guides you in the dark times when you have low to no visibility?
- How do you navigate options that don't have guaranteed outcomes or predictable circumstances?

The answer to all of these questions is the same, values. Know your values. Your values are your beacon, your lighthouse, your GPS system providing direction. Strong values provide answers often before we even ask the questions.

Life provides many forks in the road where decisions have immediate and often long-lasting repercussions. For some individuals, making an important decision is almost paralyzing because there are not clear-cut, black and white choices to choose between. Choices often have serious pros and cons, and come in various shades of gray, making things confusing and hard to distinguish. Most of us have some strong feelings about what we believe in (our values), but we have not taken the time to arrange or rank them according to what we consider most important. I call this value order.

Once you have a more clearly defined value order, decision-making becomes less of a struggle. It becomes more straightforward and streamlined. I can hear the rebuttals already, "Some decisions need a long time to process," and "I don't want to rush things," etc. The length of time it takes you to make a decision flows in direct proportion to how connected you are with your value order.

Your value order is as unique to you as your fingerprints. I am fascinated with how our fingerprints are one of a kind. There are similar patterns but no two are identical. Our fingerprints were formed during our time in the womb. The way our amniotic fluid swished and swirled over time created the tiny ridges on our fingertips. What is so amazing to me is how nearly invisible and insignificant the texture is, yet it is capable of revealing the identity of its owner.

Think about that in terms of your value order imprint. It is something that identifies and characterizes you and I. Where I have touched something, I have left my mark. When we live an authentic life, achieving the dreams placed inside our hearts by our Creator, we will leave our fingerprint behind. There are qualities, personal standards, a spirit of excellence and integrity (mixed with a lot of humor) that I hope are the identifying imprint I would leave behind anywhere I invest myself.

If I were to mimic others in their values, my individual print would be undetectable and have no additional impact. It is when you clearly define and live your values that your personal fingerprint gains true distinction.

CHAPTER ONE

1

525,600 MINUTES

MISSING OUT

Early one morning the phone rang. It was unusual to receive a call before school, so I knew something had to be up. Our nanny answered and said, "Charity, it's for you."

"This is certainly unexpected," I thought. I stopped getting ready for school and picked up the phone. "Hello?" I said, waiting to see who was on the other end of the line. "Mom! Is that you?" I was so excited to talk to her.

Looking back, I can't even remember what city she called me from. At that time my parents travelled all over the world. They worked for my grandparents, Charles and Frances Hunter, as part of their ministry. I remember my mom suddenly got very quiet.

"Are you okay?" I asked, sensing something was wrong.

On the other end of the line, I could tell she was crying. She could hardly get anything more out than a tear-filled squeak. All kinds of thoughts began racing through my head of what news she had to share with me. Did someone die? Was there a wreck? Is my dad okay? "Mom? What is it?" I asked.

"Honey, everything is fine," she answered softly.

"Then why are you sad?" I challenged.

"Mommy and Daddy won't be able to be at your 6th grade graduation ceremony tonight." I heard her suck in her breath as she finished, quieting more tears.

This was no real surprise because they were out of town. Still I had hoped they might surprise me ... really hoped. Up until that moment when she said they couldn't come I hadn't realized just how much. I tried to console her because when she felt sad it made me feel sad.

"Mom, I understand. I know you can't help it. Your job makes you have to miss things." I tried not to cry or even sound too disappointed, wanting to be strong. I knew this wasn't her fault and I didn't want to make her feel any worse than she already did.

We talked for a few more minutes before I hung up and went to school. It was a pretty normal day of class, but in the middle of the day a man came to our classroom to make a delivery. He had a vase with red roses in it—six to be exact. My teachers were both male so I knew they were not the recipients. Plus flower delivery in school was not something we had ever really seen before. "Who are they for?" was on everybody's mind. It was exciting!

My teacher stood up to greet the delivery man, "Well," he said, "and who might these beautiful roses be for?"

The man looked at the card and said, "Charity."

"What?" I looked up, but was sure I had heard him wrong.

"These are for Charity," he repeated.

"OH MY GOSH" I said, beaming. I had never received flowers before. I couldn't believe these were for me!

The huge spray of flowers was brought to my school desk. They eclipsed everything in all their glory. I didn't even know what to say!

"Read the card," my teacher instructed, smiling.

Card? I didn't even know these things had cards. It said, "Happy 6th Grade Graduation. We are so proud of you!"

They were from my parents! "Wow," I thought, "How cool is this?"

That night our small school held the graduation ceremony in a meeting room at Luby's Cafeteria. Fancy, right? Don't be jealous. In lieu of being there themselves, my parents sent a friend who was a videographer along with several other friends to come in their stead and cheer for me. I probably had more people there for me than any other student. I was voted "Most Likely to Star in 'One Flew Over the Cuckoo's Nest'" ... as the cuckoo, of course. Following all the awards and recognitions, we were each handed our diplomas and then dismissed to go home. My parents' friends all hugged me and gave their congratulations, most adding something like, "I know your mom and dad really wanted to be here."

I had no doubt of that, but it still hurt a little. A very different kind of hurt. One that I kept inside for a long time. This moment in my childhood was significant. Many things about me were shaped by what that moment represented to me. I was missing my parents, and they were missing out on this important-to-me milestone. My mom had gone above and beyond to demonstrate her support for me and show me how much she cared by sending a team of ambassadors to carry the message, but it wasn't the same.

What part of what happened was really within their control? Could they have done something to change the scenario, but didn't? Did they have to work because of the bills they had (results of choices they made)? Were they under pressure from their employers—my grandparents—who expected a great deal from them? Was there a fear of disappointing fellow staff? My sixth grade self was incapable of knowing the big picture in that moment. I know they tried their best. I honor them for trying to fill their absence from me with thoughtful things and other people. But, had I ever been given the option, I would have taken having them there over all the other stuff any day.

I had skipped fifth grade. Graduating sixth grade was major in my mind. I had done it! I had skipped fifth grade and conquered sixth with my head held high. I did not fail ... I was so proud and wanted them to be proud of me. I had never ever met anyone who had skipped a grade before. My hero of the day was Wonder

Woman. Skipping fifth grade and graduating from sixth meant, like her, I too had super human intelligence. Surely my parents wouldn't want to miss that!

My young mind struggled to make the connections. I could see the relationship between the bills we had as a family and the time my parents had to be away. I would ration certain foods—like pancake syrup—because, "If we didn't have to buy syrup again for a while, that would save money and they wouldn't have to work so much or be away so long." I would get angry at my sisters if I saw them leave excess syrup on their plates, because when they wasted it, that meant it was going to cost more money and my mom and dad would have to work more. To alleviate stress and try to make more time available with mom and dad, I would clean and help around the house. I became quite industrious in hopes that my parents time could be spent on our family.

THE ABSENCE OF PRESENCE

It is possible to occupy the same space with a person and have them not be with you. You can be in the same house with someone who is not present. Apart from all the traveling my dad did, even when he was home, he was emotionally absent for the most part. I was unaware, but for most of my parent's marriage, my dad was living in a state of inner conflict. His behavior was unusual and did not make any sense. I often felt disappointed that he didn't want to be with us more and wondered if I had done something to make him upset. It wasn't until after my parents divorced that I learned my father was homosexual. All I knew at the time was that even when he was home with us, he still wasn't with us.

My father would often be the one to pick us up from school. As soon as we were home he would retreat to his bedroom for hours while Mom was still at work. Occasionally, I would slip in there to talk to him or ask a question, but he would get angry. He would slam his computer cabinet door shut and shout, "Get out! Wait for Mom to get home ... ask her!"

This went on for years. He lived with us. We were a family under one roof, but dad was absent—completely unavailable to us. Now as an adult, I know what he was doing at his computer, and can understand what he didn't want me seeing. But the damage from the absence of his presence was done.

This pattern of deferring us to our mom continued on through my college years. I would call home a couple of times a week to check-in and if he answered, it would always be, "Let me get your mom on the phone." Thankfully she was always eager to hop on and talk. She listened too. Over time I had enough of him just putting me aside and sending me to her, and I discontinued my pursuit of a relationship with him. His actions made me assume he didn't want one anyways.

Absence of presence is not a phenomenon exclusive to adults. It runs rampant today as early as pre-teens. It seems like everywhere you go, people have earbuds in or headphones on, isolating themselves, displaying that they desire to be left alone, undisturbed, and disconnected. It is obvious there is someplace else they would rather be, doing something else with someone else. Every new device that comes on the market seems to have more apps, more music, more games, and more interactive, individualized entertainment for us to engage our time with. Cable went from eleven channels to thousands. If we are ever bored, we can immediately jump into an alternate reality, or visit someone else's reality and be whisked away out of our own life.

Out of the ashes of absenteeism, one direct consequence that arises is the lack of connection people are experiencing. Intimacy (knowing and being known) is no longer the fabric of friendships and relationships. It is more like stalking and being stalked. We think we know someone by their social media feed, we even call ourselves friends, but in reality a face-to-face conversation would be awkward. This kind of voyeuristic behavior actually bankrupts life experiences and flesh and blood relationships.

Have you ever thought how strange it is that our culture wants to use/spend/waste their time watching celebrities or other random people live their lives? What an insane exchange for our time—spending any portion of our life watching someone else live theirs! Cravings for that kind of entertainment are based on a deficiency in personal experiences or validation of their own personal use of time. People who chronically live vicariously through others don't recognize it happening. It starts a cycle of feeling alone, missing out, envy, jealousy, ... an overall curse of comparison and disconnection. Rather than take responsibility for their actions, they blame their feelings of disconnection on their schedule, their job, their children, their lack of children, anything and everyone else but themselves. Absenteeism is easily cured. A decision to become present is all it takes. But even though absenteeism is a reversible behavior, time lost is irreplaceable. The collateral relational damage created by a lack of presence will require careful and intentional mending.

MY PRECIOUS

The most valuable resource any of us has is time. We all were truly created equal in that we each have 24 hours in a day, 168 hours or 10,080 minutes a week. We are each granted the gift of 525,600 minutes a year to live.

> **The most valuable resource any of us has is time**

Let's say you slept an average of eight hours per night for a weekly average of 56 hours. That leaves 112 awake hours per week. Subtract the 40+ hours of work and work related activities (like commuting, getting ready and travel or training). What's left? About six hours a day during the work week, and roughly 32 hours across the weekend to define yourself. How you spend these minutes, ultimately, defines your values.

We can measure out what we value in minutes. The value of something in your life is determined by the amount of time it takes to attain it or the amount of time you give to it. It is a cut and dried system; one based on actions and not words alone. When I ask my children, "How do you know I love you?" Their response is not, "Because you said you love me." It is based on actions that require me to spend my time with them. For example, my son knows I love him when I play games with him or help him with school. My Kate knows I love her when I do her hair or watch her dance moves. There is even the occasional group trip to a pool or park where I can communicate love and value to all of them at once, SCORE! Your value order, put simply, is the intentional allocation of your time.

ACTION POINT

One way to discover some of your broad core values would be to ask yourself the question, "What would I do if I had only six months to a year left to live?"

- List the first five to ten things that come to mind.

- List the people who flash in your mind as well.

- Once you have your list made, ask yourself, "What do all these things have in common?"

I bet the common denominator among them all is that they are ways to SPEND your TIME! With the thought of a short window of life left, the value of your time just increased. It increased because the quantity became in limited supply. Things in limited supply get special treatment and special consideration. If you want to execute maximized value for your minutes, knowing what matters will allow for strategic planning to get the job done!

The harsh reality is that most of us live as if we have all the time in the world. We don't mind wasting our time in lines waiting for the newest Jordans, phones, laptops, movies, restaurants, roller coasters, gift with purchases, Black Friday sales, and limited edition things. We don't mind spending excess amounts of time checking facebook, playing Xbox®, or watching the hours of shows stored on the DVR. We don't mind wasting time thinking or worrying about what people—whom we don't really care about and who don't care about us—think. We don't mind working more hours to make more money to buy a bigger house we will hardly ever see because we are constantly working to keep it.

When you shift your thoughts on your time to how truly valuable it is, you become less and less tolerant of any waste. The more I remain true to doing things consistent with my value order, the more freely I enjoy the fruits of those choices. A personal example for me and many other authors is we value getting a message out in the form of a book. Well, anyone can want to write a book, but the time must be allocated. For me to allocate time for a book means that I must take that time from one of my other values until it is complete. In writing season, the value order shifts to make time to write. The reallocation process is not so much a formal one, but one where I have a daily writing goal and a weekly word count goal that get met before I get to the defragmenters like watching a favorite show or relaxing.

The closer I hold myself to these goals, the more satisfying the relaxation is. Reason being, my mind isn't gnawing at me the whole time I am pretending to be totally into the other activity. Darn that conscience sometimes! You know what I mean though, it's knowing you got your workout in, knowing you spent quality time with your family or friends, knowing you gave work 100% while you were on the clock, knowing you nurtured your spirit, knowing the laundry and dishes are done ... that make relaxation the most powerful.

The disconnect for many is knowing they should relax and rest, but do not because they don't see its purpose or value, they don't calculate its benefits. Rest is not waste if done in the proper proportion to gainful working, home, and personal maintenance. Rest is NOT relaxing while doing something else. There is no multi-tasking involved in rest. Rest means "to cease work or movement in order to relax, refresh oneself, or recover strength." Most of us place very little to no value on rest. We see it as laziness when in reality, it is restorative. It is both healthy and mandatory. Because of today's demanding pace, you must be intentional about it. I heard one of my friends describe what she and her husband call "protecting the white space" on their calendar. I'm sure she didn't invent that phrase, but it was the first time I had heard it and it had a big impact on me. Protecting is exactly right. You must guard a certain percentage of your life for rest.

ONE YEAR TO LIVE

So, let's return to the thought of having only one year to live. I asked several of my friends and family to tell me what they came up with. Here are some of their answers:

- "I would rearrange my time to spend it with those I love."
- "I wouldn't eat healthy ... I would enjoy life."
- "I would spend some money on experiences."

- "I would write in my Bible so my children could see what I wrote and I would either do a video journal or a written journal for my family."

- "I would make sure I did all I could to set my wife up financially ...

- "I would spend my time more purposefully and not waste it."

- "I would write a book or a movie—I have a message inside me that I would want to get out and leave behind before I go."

- "I would give to charitable causes and go on a big trip. Other than that, nothing really would change. I love what I do and would continue to do it."

One common response to my question was actually, "I don't know." For some, this ambiguous response came from being unfamiliar with their values. For others, it came from already living their values and the not knowing if they would change a thing. For myself, I would probably say that if I had one year left to live, I would do things like:

- Take my family on a big trip or two or five.

- Enjoy everything.

- Take tons of pictures.

- Write my husband and children letters for their future enjoyment.

- Spend one on one time with my immediate family.

- Take a girls' trip with my mom and sisters somewhere with pools and beaches.

- Do my best to create wonderful memories that will be with my family forever.

- Buy each of my children a nice watch so that every time they looked at it they would be anchored knowing it was from me.

Each of these desires has a root to it, a way to deconstruct the noise and complexity of it and see what is really valued. My number one value is to do everything with purpose and do it well. It is likely that I would strategize a plan to get everything in, possibly exacerbating some of it due to the amount of chaos that would bring. I would then have to remind myself to relax and remember to enjoy rather than stress away these precious moments. I would probably be seen with no makeup, my hair in a pony tail, clothes I could move around in, a camera around my neck at all times, and my favorite flip flops. Why? Because I wouldn't care to spend any of my time on dressing up. I would just be me and be perfectly okay with that. The beauty of establishing your own value order is that no one else has permission or power to influence you into valuing anything different. It gives you solid ground to stand on, and anchors your actions to your values.

To help you start hammering out your value order, let's start by looking at several large topics, and then break them down as we go. At the center of this visual diagram is a circle with "Time" written in it. Imagine it is like the sun emitting light all around it. Radiating from the center circle are lines at various lengths with value words at the end of them. The closer the value word is to the center, the higher the value because it receives the most light (or time). The value words that are further from the center receive the residual. Certain values overlap. Some values prevent others from getting any time. This would be one of those either or situations where you had to commit to one value even if both are favorable or unfavorable.

Here is a short list of things we value that you can use to prompt your value order. By no means do these have to be included in yours if they don't apply. This list is just to help you start thinking.

- Career
- Home Maintenance
- Spouse
- Children
- Family and Close Friends
- Spirituality
- Health and Personal Maintenance

This list covers the pillars of our family's value order. Once you have established your pillars and where they fall, there are some subcategories and characteristics to also put in value order. Here are a few that come to mind for me that bear a lot of weight in my decision-making process:

- Cost
- Quality
- Frustration/No Frustration

- Energy it will take to get it/ energy it will give back to me
- Enjoyment
- Meaningful
- Wasteful
- Is it the best option?
- Will doing it be in the best interest of the family?
- What is the R.O.I. (Return On Investment)?
- What opportunities are lost if we commit funds to something else?
- Is this making life better? Worse?
- What option saves me the most time without sacrificing quality?
- Easy vs. Challenging
- Convenience (Costs) vs. "Do It Yourself" (Frugality)
- You Only Live Once
- You may live a long time and should set aside _____ for that
- What do I really want my children to get out of their learning?
- Better school district or more affordable home?
- Put the baby in daycare and keep working, or stay at home and live on less?

- Is there a win/win?
- I want what he/she has.
- Individuality vs. Conformity?
- "Bigger, better, newer model ... always!" vs. "Use it until the wheels fall off!"

What you value is found in each choice you make, big or small. The more proactive you are in the discovery of your values, the sooner you can live your life in the key of you. Each choice you make has a fee associated with it that affects the balance of your time positively or negatively. It is the ultimate currency you get to decide how to spend and truthfully, it is in limited supply.

One thing I learned as I was in the writing process of this book is the benefit of an outline. I wrote the first 14,000 words in a stream of consciousness fashion based off of a bubble sheet I had made. It was difficult and had me concerned that I would repeat myself, or not have any flow to the logic or story. I was also at a point where life was so hectic with Ted's schooling I put the book away for a while to get everything done I needed to. Whenever I would think to go back and continue, I would hesitate because if I wasn't writing well, I would stop and enlist a ghost writer to help. I can't stand the thought of wasting time, so away it remained. A few month after I stopped, I handed what I had to my editor. I told her, I needed her help and expertise to see if it was worth completing. Months and many life changes later, we reconnected and she encouraged me to continue, and that what I had was worth me finishing. We spent two days spreading it all out and forming an outline. What a difference an outline made in the pace I was able to finish the book in!

I now knew where I was going and why. It made staying on topic and staying the course much easier. I had taken the time to hammer out the details. With the help of a resource, I could see from a fresh perspective and ask questions to help me articulate the true message I wanted to convey. This concept of an outline or a roadmap is what this book can help you achieve for your life. Your value order will function like a filter, keeping things that are important and letting go of things that aren't. Each decision you face once you know your value order, can filter through and land exactly where it will bring you the most satisfaction. This journey is worth the effort and time it will take you to complete. It is the faster way once it is finished.

ACTION POINT

- Write down your value order pillars. They don't have to be in your final (for now) order.

- Next to them, list a few of the reasons why you have them where you do and revisit the list in a week.

Remember your value order will evolve as your life evolves. Today's value order is not forever, it's just for now, so don't put too much pressure for perfection on your first draft. Sometimes the most difficult steps are the first. I like to know as much as possible about a situation before I start something new. I saw a sign one night as I was driving home, and at the time I was in a personal whirlwind. We were a few months away from packing up our wonderful life in Nashville to head to Houston. There were so many unknowns and "what-ifs." The sign simply said, "You don't have to know it all, to begin." If you are anything like me, defining your values may seem like laying out cement so you must get it right. That's not the case. While values are important and will have a vast impact on your life, allow yourself the freedom to begin where you are right now ... before you know it all.

CHAPTER TWO

2

O.P.V.

OTHER PEOPLE'S VALUES

• •

Navigating your value order journey should be simple right? It is. But when you learn that your values aren't the only ones out there, it becomes a bit more complicated. There are a myriad of other values and causes speaking loudly and shining brightly that can make it difficult to find or recognize YOUR way. We all have values. We share some and others polarize us. People make judgments of others based on how they look through their own lens. This lens of personal values highlights things that are different about others. Then, depending on their location on this journey, how they handle these differences can be quite diverse. This reliance upon our own lens and how it applies to others is why there is so much misunderstanding in the world. Our value order lens will not mirror another person's decisions exactly—even inside the same family—therefore this is foolish to expect. Conformity is for the insecure. It is a comfortable place to disappear and provides a false sense of security. Establishing yourself and your value order should give you a good nudge out of conformity's nest.

I was sharing with one of my clients who was about to have a baby, that whatever she decided to do for her baby, someone who did not make that same choice would feel the need to defend their choice to her. For example, if she chose not to return to work, a mother who did return to work would want to explain why she did. If she decided to use disposable diapers, the cloth-diapering mother would want to explain the pros of doing what she did. Each decision we make, big or small, is a statement of our values. But the statement isn't about condemning those around you, it is about writing your own story and holding fast to your values. The sooner you become less influenced by people just seeking your agreement with them, the sooner your life will flow in the direction of your dreams and your purpose.

LOOKING THROUGH A LENS

People are funny. I love to people-watch, especially long-term watching. One of my favorite behaviors to observe is the war within between wanting to feel like part of a herd and wanting to stand out as an individual. The more decisive the person, the shorter the war, but it is entertaining to observe none-the-less. I enjoy being around decisive people. I don't have to agree with everything they are about, but the fact that they can move forward based on an inner conviction of and connection to their values is pleasant to be around. But, be honest, for each of us there are "types" of people that can drive us nuts. As you begin to discover and stand on your values, you will notice these and other types of people around you who do not share the same passion or conviction. They may live in your house, be in the next cubicle, or possibly present at every family function. See if any of these sound familiar.

THE INDECISIVE PERSON

Can you think of someone you know who always seems stuck? They are constantly waffling back and forth between two radically similar options with no progress ever actually being made. The khakis or the slightly darker khakis? The chicken sandwich or the chicken wrap? Latte or macchiato? Forget even mentioning the choice of paint color for any wall of their house!

Ted and I have been married for a while now, and for the most part he is a decisive person. But one thing that still makes me smile about him is his decision making process when we go out to a restaurant. I know that when the server comes back to our table and asks if we are ready to order, I will be ready, and he will think he is. I will tell them my order and Ted will instantly go into a brief but hilariously painful-to-watch panic mode. It appears as if he has never seen the menu, and has no recollection of where we are or how we got there. If in a pinch, he will quickly locate the steak section and ask for the ribeye. It may not be what he originally thought about getting, but it will work. To prevent these situations, I try to ask him in advance what he wants so I can help him out if he needs me to. I really am entertained by this, and it is endearing.

The indecisive person deals with this "panic of the decision" all the time, not just at meals. You can count on them to be a definite maybe on your invite list. They must poll the audience in search of the popular vote. They must search the internet to find enough conflicting evidence about every topic until they believe there are no real answers in the world. They are afraid of making the wrong decision to the point they make no decisions. This lack of confidence is paralyzing and stunts many a destiny. Think about the couple that have been dating for eight years. He is just not sure if she's "the one." "Could I do better?" he wonders, "Is her mother a part of the package? Will her father really kill me if I break up with her? Sometimes I get bored. Does that mean I should get out?" She stays because of all the years she has invested in the relationship, yet she is still on the bubble. The indecisive types are not well connected to their values and their value order in a way that permits them to be bold.

Another way to spot the indecisive type is they tend to run late. They have stood at their closet waiting for the right outfit to speak to them ... not realizing fifteen minutes went by. Next they stared at the food in the pantry hoping that some new way to make oatmeal would pop in their head. With the challenge of breakfast at last behind them, they stared at the things to bring with them, pondering how far into the day they should pack their car for feeling uncertain about all the "what ifs" that could arise. By the time they get the car packed and start to back out of the driveway, they notice the clock on the dashboard, realize they are running late, then frantically try to come up with (and stick with) a reasonable excuse that will be believable. Did I mention the five minutes they loved on their sweet four-legged family member, writhing in the guilt they felt about leaving him home alone all day ... wondering, "Should I consider doggy daycare?"

They likely have values buried in their Mary Poppins-like carpetbag somewhere. They simply don't know how to access their value order, therefore they remain where they are indefinitely. Indecisive people are hard for me to be around. When I worked in the music business as a talent agent, we had one concert promoter who always "talked about booking" one or more of our artists. In my four years in the business, our agency spoke with this promoter regularly and the conversations were positive. He always seemed interested and would schedule a follow up call for us to remind him of certain dates and so forth. But at the end of the day, he NEVER booked anyone. What a waste of time and energy! Time and energy are the currency of life. When you waste time and energy you are wasting your life.

They don't know how to access their value order, therefore they remain where they are indefinitely

Talking about doing things is powerful, inoculating even. It causes the brain to feel as though you have actually done what you are saying. Your brain rewards you with the same feel-good chemical reactions you would get if you actually did those things. Have you ever experienced this? I have. At different times in my life, I wanted to begin something new or change something. When I discussed the desire to change and the possible plan of attack with friends and family, I rarely experienced success. When

I kept it virtually to myself and just focused on the changing, I had more traction and long-term success.

Whenever I come across people who do a lot of "talking about doing things," I generally try to get as far away as possible. In my younger and less filtered days, I felt compelled to point out the fact that they were all talk no action. The older I get, the more I realize that even pointing that out is often a waste of energy. These folks are not doers. They love to be around those who are. Until they are able to own the fact that their life has been but a pile of words, do not try to push a talker to action. If you are ready to move forward in your life, my best advice is to avoid long periods of time with them. Do not give them a voice in your life.

THE YOUNG AND DUMB PERSON

Second is the "young and dumb" person. You know who they are—the high school senior thinking they are at the top of the heap of life, the first year resident, the newlywed ... they feel invincible, hence the need to be very vocal. They are the first to spout off in almost every situation, revealing to anyone around that they have no long term experience yet. They have very high standards for everyone that they have had no chance to demonstrate in their own life.

One of my favorite examples of this young and dumbness happened when I was working retail, just after college. I was around 22 years old with no responsibilities outside of myself. I worked, worked out, and hung out with friends. Oh, the life! One day, I had a female customer come in to shop with me. She was trying to find some clothes and was having some challenges. I was ready and happy to help her in her quest. After about thirty minutes of us working together and making some progress, she said, "I just had a baby but haven't lost the baby-weight yet."

I said, "Oh fun! You have a baby? How old is your baby?"

"Eighteen months," she answered.

In my head, I was like, "EIGHTEEN MONTHS? You didn't JUST have a baby! That kid is coming up on college!" I judged this woman based on how her situation looked through my inexperienced lens. All I could see was a lazy, unmotivated, procrastinating whiner. Fast-forward six years to when I was pregnant in my first trimester, with my first child. I told one of my friends (who had adult children of her own) that any weight I gained during pregnancy I was going to lose in the first three months after the baby was born. I was not going to skip a beat with my workouts once I was cleared for them. Then bing, bang, boom be back in my pre-pregnancy clothes in no time!

... Now, about that first trimester ... I was very nauseous, for what seemed like forever. Nothing smelled good, much less tasted good. So like most people who go ten weeks or more without being able to eat anything, the moment I felt better I was ready to eat! I didn't gain any weight my first trimester so I was feeling pretty good about the fact that I probably wouldn't gain very much at all outside of the bare minimum. Six months, forty pounds and an emergency c-section following a long "natural" labor later, I had my son. Ted and I were officially sent into the outer realms of being mind-blowingly tired while being family-less in Nashville. Everything was harder than I could have ever imagined. Feeding a baby every two-and-a-half hours, remembering to feed myself, diapers, blow-out diapers, me crying, the baby crying, recovering from surgery, drinking enough water to hopefully be able to have a bowel movement that day, piles of laundry, a yard to mow ... oh, and run a business and work a part-time job! It made three months seem like a week. I remember looking at the scale around the three-month mark. I was still about forty pounds up with no baby in my belly thinking, "I should not have thought all of those mean thoughts about that woman all those years ago." With the lens of personal experience I could then easily see how 18 months could feel like one just had a baby. I don't think I felt like I had a moment to spare until he was around six or seven months old, and even then I felt I owed those spare moments to my husband. It wasn't until Luke was just over eighteen months that I really started to make time for myself and get focused on my health again.

The phrase "young and dumb" is more accurately described as "ignorant." Ignorant isn't the same thing as dumb. Dumb is a choice, whereas ignorance is a lack of experience or information. The benefit of being around an inexperienced person is that in a lot of areas they are fearless. They are bold and militant. If you find you may be in this category from time to time, the key will be to hit the mute button. A fool is most often exposed by his words. So even if you say nothing at all, people will perceive you as smarter than you probably are.

Smack dab in the middle of the inexperienced category is one of my personal favorites, the D.I.N.K. If you don't know what a D.I.N.K. is, it stands for Dual Income, No Kids. They are in the family of the inexperienced, and such a fun group to spotlight. This "well-meaning" yet naive group definitely makes sure their values are seen and heard. They don't understand why you can't afford to go out for a night out on the town because they have no idea that babysitting costs are ridiculous these days. They are the couple on the plane that give you the less than pleasant looks when your child is crying because they assume you can't control your child. They have strong feelings about how you should vaccinate your child. If your child was theirs, they would not allow them to have sugar. Their children would never be seen with stains on their clothes, especially in public. They would also never go out in public themselves unless they were put together. They prey upon moms and dads who have just let themselves go in the name of child-rearing and its sometimes demanding schedule. They laugh at their parent friends when they see them get tired by 8:30 p.m. because they are not as young as they used to be.

The D.I.N.K. type occurs in other areas as well. They are unqualified experts that feel their voice is worth listening to. They can make you second guess every choice you make. They will rattle off the latest article they read which had a buzzword that relates to you in it and let their venom sink in. The thing to remember is what is right today by the experts, may not be right tomorrow. I had four children in eight and a half years. When my first child was born, the "medical experts" told me there was a certain way that my baby should sleep for prevention of SIDS and other various sleep hazards. By the time I had my last child, that "way" had changed a couple of times. Why did it change? I'm sure it was a mix of new information and new opinions, but mostly more time and

Unqualified "experts" love to voice their opinion about everything

experience. When I look back at the pictures of when my parents brought me home from the hospital (not THAT long ago), there was no rear-facing infant car seat with five-point harness system and a frame locked plural seat or base. My mom held me, in her loving arms, the whole way home. There were no airbags in the car ... I don't even know if she even buckled her lap belt! Today, if this scenario happened and a police officer saw it, there would be a laundry list of violations, an expensive ticket, and possibly child endangerment charges brought to the person who would ever put a baby in harm's way like that. Do your best and don't worry about the rest, especially the voice of the ignorant.

The statement, "Ignorance is bliss," is really only cute when it refers to children. Some of the best content I get daily is from my children. It is always amusing to hear what they think because they are a pretty clean slate and have no filters. Their opinions are not based on anything but imagination and a couple of the most recent movies they have seen. They possess infinite bravado and unlimited time in their own minds, so of course nothing seems impossible. It is only as they, like us all, grow up to know their limits that the filters come into play. By limits I don't mean things we can't do, but rather things that we choose not to do because there isn't enough time in the day and cloning ourselves hasn't really happened yet.

THE "BEEN THERE, DONE THAT" PERSON

Third is the "experienced" type. When you tell them something you have begun, especially in the area of self-improvement, their response is something like, "I've tried that before, and it doesn't work." It is amazing how many experts and critics emerge when you have made a decision to improve yourself or your condition. They will try to help you foresee into the future, "When the excitement and thrill is gone and you return to the herd with your tail tucked ... " ... it will, of course, be because you fell prey to the same pitfalls they did.

One of my friends and her family are vegan. This wasn't a decision they made because of a fad or series of hip documentaries. Her husband fought and won a serious battle with cancer and she researched the best food regimen for them and their family has stuck with it. They don't walk around with "I'm vegan. Ask me" shirts on, or hand out PETA tracks. They simply are vegan. Now as soon as anyone asks something smart like, "Where's the beef?" they answer truthfully that they are vegan. Wouldn't you know that the next question is, "Well, how do you get your protein?" They, like many other good vegans, shake their heads and laboriously list a few top sources, but are often stared back at with a look a shock and disbelief. This protein question is a silly example, but you know what I mean.

You have met the kind of people I am talking about. If you begin working out, they will ask if you wear tennis shoes or go barefoot? Low carb? Low calorie? Cabbage soup? Paleo? You can recognize these people because they do not reflect or resemble the value you are aiming for despite how much they talk about it. They are also the ones offering you cookies, cakes, cokes, and beer if they know you are trying to be disciplined. If you cave, they celebrate internally like the witch who got Snow White to bite the apple. Beware. Their intention is not to simply encourage you to let yourself have a single treat or cheat once in a while. They want to begin your path back to a level playing field with them. Misery loves company. It is a great idea to turn up the volume of the voices of those who live out the value you are developing.

THE ELITIST

The next type of person is the overbearing type. They characteristically bulldoze their values with a "My way is best, so fall in line," attitude. If you dare disagree with an elitist you are considered uneducated or behind on the times. These people believe and have conviction in their values (good or bad), but often lack mercy, perspective, and/or people skills to temper them. Being from Dallas, my husband and I are Dallas Cowboy fans for life. Now, I know that that statement alone has many of you excited or up in arms because you are either a fan of America's team or you are ... not. Either way, you can easily find the elitist when someone has a favorite team and is an obnoxious fanatic about it. The elitist loves to argue and wear people down. They don't see any of it as a waste of energy. In fact, if you don't move, they will keep talking. The elitist loves to body block or trap the other person by their body language. You will also notice they never lose control of the conversation.

Maybe you know a person who has to tell you all the time about how organic they are or how cross-fit is the only true fitness program on the planet. They might tell you what school district is the only acceptable one if you want a half-decent education for your children. They can tell you the best travel sports team to have them in, IF there is any room. The overbearing type loves to ramble on about the statistics of their 401k, their grill, their phone, even what social media they are "so over" and why you should be too.

Perhaps you have an overbearing parent who had your life mapped out for you before you were born. They knew what sports you were going to play, what college you were going to attend, and what you were going to do for a living. Any choice you made that followed their direction was praised, while any decision outside of it was discouraged and difficult. This strong-arming and manipulative personality—especially from an authority figure—often produces the indecisive type. When every decision has been made for you, it can handicap your decision making abilities.

The elitist is concerned about keeping up appearances. They want respect sprinkled with a dash of envy from others. They enjoy having just enough information to make them dangerous. They would rather be served than serve every day of the week. Oddly enough, they attract many because of their demonstrative expressions of their values. For some, this is potentially a fatal attraction because the overbearing type loves to make replicas. There may be little to nothing left of you if you spend too much time allowing this type to influence you.

THE ENABLER

The definition of enabler, according to Merriam-Webster, is, "One who enables another to achieve an end; especially: one who enables another to persist in self-destructive behavior by providing excuses or by making it possible to avoid the consequences of such behavior." We all know an enabler and those they enable. Ones that come to my mind are the mothers who cleaned up every mess their child made even into their adulthood, or the friend that will always bail their friends out financially. The enabler might even be a spouse who does everything for their partner in search for the tiniest bit of respect and approval. The enabler's selfish desire to not stir things up or keep the peace becomes destructive when it permits the other person to continue in hurtful or even harmful behavior.

We had a situation like this occur in our family. I will do my best to tell the story as anonymously as possible to protect the progress we have made. One Christmas (of course it took place at a holiday), we all got together and when that happens, there are a lot of people to accommodate. A couple of people were in charge of the meal planning and preparation. The plan was that the others would clean up or help wrangle children as their contribution to the whole process. One portion of the family had a pattern of not helping out and it was silently driving the other members up the wall. One of those more inclined to pitch in asked a parent to mention to the under-participating members that they should do dishes after Christmas dinner. After all, those members would never say no to the parent, so this would be the way to make it the least aggressive and least awkward, right?

When dinner was nearly over, the sound of dishes being done was heard ... but by the parent, not the "under-helpers." What happened next became known as the "Emotional Bowel Movement of 2013." Years of unspoken frustrations and hurt feelings came flooding out uncontrollably. The unsuspecting recipients of the comments were blindsided and ganged up on, so naturally they retaliated with fury. When everything simmered down and apologies were exchanged, we all felt better. More than feeling better, we were better. The enabling that had been going on for years had put a wedge in between members of our family. I am happy to report that holidays and get togethers since have gone much smoother, and I am so thankful.

Each of these types of personalities possesses potential for good. If their powers were refined and they became aware of what specific situations called for, their "bend" could actually provide wisdom rather than discouragement, cautious thought rather than immobility, and motivation rather than exclusion. The indecisive personality could bring benefit to an overly impulsive decision maker. They could benefit from a personality that calls them to action and helps them weigh out the choices. The experienced personality can bring benefit to someone who is at the beginning of various life stages and needs to know the cost benefit analysis of their options. They could benefit from someone who is willing to try something again or something new despite past failures or negative outcomes. An elitist can bring benefit to the drifter or the uninspired. They, in turn, could benefit from the open-minded or experienced veteran of life. Heighten your awareness to the people who surround you and pay attention to how they might be influencing you.

Each personality type possesses potential for good

I admit I have been each of these types a time or two in my life. I am a passionate person with a penchant for efficiency and frugality. I don't like to waste time, so if I tried something and it didn't work, I used to assume it wouldn't work for others. I felt it my duty to tell them that to save them time, etc. I am wired to problem solve. To some, these traits of mine have left the bad taste of an abrasive, opinionated, control seeking, bossy type. To others, they translated as a leader—savvy, economical, and smart. I am just as passionate as ever and wired the same way, but experience, time, and life have taught me a better way to deliver my goods.

THE TRUE FRIEND

We have talked about many of the negative types out there, but then there is the one that we hope to find and hope to be: the true friend. A true friend is a confidant, a companion. They do not desire to be in competition with those they spend time with. They are comfortable in who they are and in who their friends are.

A true friend will bring out the best in you and allow you to bring it out in them

One of the best things about a true friend is they will bring out the best in you and allow you to do the same for them. They want what is best for you and are willing to walk through your consequences with you rather than help you run from them. They provide a healthy perspective and offer wisdom rather than comfort. They speak the truth through the filter of love which doesn't mean sugar-coating it.

The Urban Dictionary defines friends as, "People who are aware of how retarded you are and still manage to be seen in public with you." How many of us are thankful for the true friends who are keenly aware of our flaws and weaknesses and still see not only our current value, but also our potential. The true friend tells you when you are being strung along by a boyfriend or girlfriend ... and will also be there for you when you finally call it off. A true friend will encourage your success and not try to diminish it even if it happens prior to theirs. Henry Thoreau said, "Friends ... they cherish one another's hopes. They are kind to one another's dreams." Have you ever told someone a dream of yours and they proceeded to tell you all the reasons why it probably won't happen? You can now confirm they were not a true friend. A true friend will have sage advice and know right when to give it.

WHO ARE THEY?

Now that we have exposed several types of people we may find in our midst, take the time and identify who these may be in your life. It is important to see where their values are coming from and how they relate to you. As you peel the onion back layer by layer, you may see threads of their influence woven into your own values. Some you may want there, some you may not. Recognizing their presence is powerful and gives you the ability to edit once again.

As you go through this process of discovering and possibly even modifying your values and your value order, things will naturally begin to shift in your life. These realignments are exciting, and our natural tendency is to want to tell everyone that we are actually doing something positive in our lives. I am all for you sharing the fact that you are reading the book and taking the journey, but be selective with whom you share the details of your value order. There is a good chance even your best friend will have differences from yours and it is tempting to conform to those we love, respect, and admire. Sometimes we are tempted to conform to the path of those we envy. The more free you are from external input on your values and value order, the more you will enjoy life once you are living based on them. It will be authentically yours. You will be able to stand your ground, look yourself in the eye, and know that your life is a product of intentional design rather than a series of reactions to the actions of others. This journey is not necessarily about changing what you do or how you do it. It is a tool to help you make choices that line up with what you value and actually hope to experience.

The Internet, social media, commercials, even magazines are like megaphones blaring different values at us. Those individuals who feel their values are the "correct" values extend zero tolerance for others. Oddly enough, they tend to be the ones with the least tolerance or acceptance calling anyone who disagrees with them judgmental and intolerant. If you are the type of person who is easily swayed away from your values, then it is important for you to monitor and control the voices of influence that have an audience with you. Avoid the media. Don't worry, you will not turn into one of the Cleavers if you do not indulge in filling your mind with value confusion from the media. The result of keeping the confusion to a minimum is easier decision making and clarity in the direction or course on which you desire to stay .

WHO AM I?

It is crucial for us to acknowledge that we may be one or more of these types to those we are around. It is possible for us to be different types to different people depending on how they make us feel. As the oldest sibling, I spent many years as the experienced type to my sisters. I wanted them to know that I knew more than they did and that I was in charge. If I was going to be blamed for anything they did wrong (since they had to have learned it from me), then I was going to be sure they didn't do anything stupid. I am sure they would confirm that they couldn't stand it. I know it is hard to look at yourself in the mirror, but submit your actions to honest examination. Are you an enabler? Do you bully people with your overbearing opinions? Do you have difficulty sticking with your convictions? Do you need to know what everyone else thinks before you know what you think? Ask yourself, "Am I a force for good or evil in the lives of those I come into contact with?"

*Keeping confusion
to a minimum
allows for clarity
and easier
decision making*

Chapter Three

3

THE BEST POLICY

BE HONEST WITH YOURSELF

To begin the process of discovering your values you must ask yourself, "What do I want out of life?" Many people are unhappy, unfulfilled, depressed, and disappointed because there is a chasm between what they want out of life and what they experience. Why is that? There are probably a number of reasons but let's look closely at a few.

After asking yourself what you want out of life and answering this question, the next one to ask is, "Am I living it?" Are you headed in the direction of your goals? Let's say that I want to have beautiful landscaping at my house. I decide this is of value to me. I want to look out at my yard and see beautiful plants producing lovely color and blooms. One approach to achieve this goal is to go to the local nursery, buy the plants, come home and put them in the ground, then diligently tend to them. This process takes a couple of hours to a couple of days depending on the amount needing to be done. Reality for a lot of people is there isn't that extra bubble of time automatically in their schedule. The inner monologue might sound something like this, "I have so much going on right now at work and this weekend there is a party for my friend ... plus a game or two I wanted to catch." Monday comes and goes and they think, "I wish there were flowers in my yard. My neighbor always has great landscaping. I want great landscaping too." Tuesday, Wednesday, Thursday are all rinse-and-repeats of Monday. Friday finally comes and it has been a rough week at work. They are exhausted. All they want to do is relax. They deserve a break don't they? Saturday is LAKE DAY! Friends, water, and grilling out are the perfect cure for the week they just had. Sunday is recover from the lake day, not to mention that the playoffs are on. Then they realize that Monday comes next and they will want to rest up for that. Blink and the season for planting is over for them that year.

No matter what they said their values were, their living betrayed their true values. The problem was that they were lying to themselves about landscaping holding great value to them. They saw their neighbor's end result and of course they want that. But do they really want to divert time or money from all of life's other activities and expenses to cultivate their landscaping? Their actions tell their values.

I picked landscaping as the example here because so much of what we hem, haw, and fuss over are things that are optional. They are things that don't make or break our life experience but can bring enjoyment or burden. Personally, I enjoy landscaping. I value it and I will explain why. It gets me outside... you know, the whole vitamin D thing. It is relaxing when I water the plants. It is instant gratification to pull weeds. It is beautiful to look at every day. My husband does not get the same fulfillment from it, but he values seeing me enjoy it so he helps with the harder parts of it. We could get by with a much lower maintenance set up, but it adds to my home-life experience so it is worth the investment. I am honest with myself when I act upon the fact that I will enjoy the fruits of the labor and conversely, I would experience regret not doing it and hear it in my head each time I saw our yard without it.

When you are honest with yourself, you increase your chances of being able to live a life that truly fulfills you. If mom and dad put the pressure on you to be a doctor or something else popular for parents to like, but it was never what you wanted to do, you have two options: 1) live a life of misery yet please your parents, or 2) pursue what is in your heart and live fulfilled. Hopefully mom and dad will come around as you live inside your zone, but if not, you won't have that terrible inner conflict because it is still your values, your authenticity, and ultimately your life.

> **When you are honest with yourself, you increase your chances of being able to live a life that truly fulfills you**

Know for what you are really willing to sacrifice. It is easy to want to value everything that seems cool or important, but everything has a price. If you are not ready to pay the price then stop lying to yourself (and probably others) by perpetuating the thought that it is a reality. Why do we have New Year's resolutions every year? Because we never stick to them for a full twelve months. We have to say again, "Okay this year I really am going to lose the weight, drink less, quit smoking, spend more time with my family, save money, and get that dream job." Quit lying. If I had the opportunity to script the best resolution, it would be, "Be more honest."

Being honest with yourself is the first step in closing the gap between what you want to happen and what you are experiencing.

GREAT EXPECTATIONS

Another reason people experience a disconnect in their lives is incorrect expectations. I am notorious for setting very high expectations and then experiencing let down or frustration when the dream/vision I had wasn't even close to attainment. It's a Clark Griswold kind of feeling where, in your head, you picture the family together at Christmas, all getting along. No fighting or pushing buttons. The lights are twinkling. The turkey is perfectly cooked and the Christmas bonus check arrived on time. Yes, this dream is noble. Yes, it is something you would want to document and share on social media. However, it is an unrealistic expectation, and when the holiday does unfold in a way that tends to happen when a bunch of family shoves themselves into one house for a week's time, you walk away feeling like it was a failure rather than a celebration and joyous occasion.

When Ted and I were first married, we were working hard to pay off debt and live below our means to set us up to start a family and maybe purchase a house and so forth. After a little less than a year of marriage, we had just reached a milestone in our financial journey. We had a tiny celebration with a dinner out and spent the next day doing some apartment cleaning and organizing. We had a few things to take to Goodwill, so we jumped in his Dodge Ram and headed that way. I remember it was a lovely day. The sun was out, we had the windows down and the music up. A few minutes down the highway, there was a loud banging noise coming from the engine area of the truck. Ted pulls over to the shoulder and turns the truck off. I am not auto savvy so I looked to him to give me an indication of just how bad things were. His look back was not reassuring. I began to cry. I know enough about cars to know that engines making sounds like that meant thousands of dollars in repairs. This was an older truck, so it may have even meant replacing it. Ted called the repair shop close to our apartment and they towed it. The rods in the engine ... blah, blah, blah ... Basically, we were going to have to replace the engine.

This was not my idea of what should be happening to two newlyweds who were trying with everything within them to pay off debt and be smart with their money. This kind of stuff happens to those who don't care and don't work hard, right? I began to rant about how this wasn't fair and how we had just celebrated the progress from our hard work and how this isn't what I imagined marriage to be like. Then Ted and I had one of the strangest conversations ever. He explained to me that when he asked me to marry him, he basically planned on the "for worse, for sicker, and for poorer," and that anything above that would be great. It was then that I realized that I had pretty much planned for or expected "for better, for health, and for richer!" I had unknowingly set my expectations up in such a way that many of our days together could have been chalked up as failure or disappointments. We then discussed how both of us probably had set incorrect expectations. Setting expectations too low can cause an unproductive attitude or at least under-productive. Setting expectations too high can put you and those around you in a permanent state of never good enough. There is a middle ground of contentment matched with the pursuit of goals and dreams.

Another cause for our life experience to not match our values is that we are not really sure what our values are. We have not taken the time to clarify, define, map out, and rank our values. This process is not a one time, done for life event. It does have a beginning and it does evolve and change at different times in our lives. The values of a single person may operate one way but then must adapt and change to include their spouse. A single person, in most cases, doesn't have to account to anyone for where they are going to be, when they will be home, how they spend their money, where they live, etc. Out of consideration and respect for their spouse, the details of their life become inclusive of the needs of the spouse and the values he or she holds as well.

Being honest with your spouse is also one of the best gifts you can give yourself. It gives you the freedom to be yourself around them all the more. Here are some scenarios that demonstrate how honesty truly is the best policy:

When whoever cooked the meal asks. "Do you like it?" Answer honestly. If you don't like and you answer that you do to prevent hurt feelings, you will eat that meal again and again.

When asked, "What do you want to do tonight?" give an honest answer with options not just a decision deferment of, "I don't know, what do you want to do?"

When making decisions about when and where to spend money and what to spend it on, honesty is crucial. You must speak up about what you want for your future and for your present.

One area where Ted and I diverge a little is that he is an over-giver and I am a recovering penny-pincher. We both love giving, we just do it in different ways. There have been times when the local churches we were members of had special causes we wanted to give to. A particular amount would come to my mind that felt like a stretch. I would ask Ted what he thought about the extravagant (for us) figure. Inevitably, he was thinking usually double or triple the amount causing mine to feel small. He would ask me how I felt about that number and I would tell him either yes, or no and explain my feelings. There were times that I would say, "I don't think that is our amount," and he would push back forcing me to become more bold on my position or to acquiesce. Because we made a promise to each other to be honest before we were even married, I have always told him the truth on how I feel—even if it means we disagree. We have a mutual respect for each other's opinion outside of the fact that he is the head of our household. I am thankful we function best when we are being honest with each other.

When children come into the picture values change again. Children have a way of making you super creative on new ways of doing things and new times of doing them so you can be around them more. I love watching die-hard career women turn into fire-breathing entrepreneurs once those little dumplings start coming. My children are a huge part of the reason I have been self-employed most of my adult life. I value being involved in as much of their lives as I can, especially while they are under my roof. I love them. I am crazy about them. Being self-employed is not the most risk-free way of life. When you are self-employed, there are no sick days and no paid time off. However, it does have many perks that I value more than I fear the risks. I was able to be honest with myself and know that I would do whatever it took business-wise to support my family and even my husband while he went through four and a half years of full-time college. Yes, several of those years were some of the hardest years of my life but it was worth the flexibility it provided me to be with my family when I needed to be.

DECIDE OR DEAL

Life will not wait for you to get your value order organized and laminated on scrapbook paper and post it on your page or wall. It mercilessly marches on. There will be repercussions for choosing and not choosing an honest value order. When you decide, it puts you behind the steering wheel. When you forgo choosing, it puts you in the back seat. You can tell the ones who live in the back seat because they are yelling, fussing, and complaining about their life and its problems because they feel out of control. They are victims subjected to the cards life dealt them. They are passive about their decisions, yet noisy with their feelings about the outcomes. Not choosing is still a choice, perhaps even the most dangerous choice. I equate it to driving with blind curve signs frequently popping up when you least expect them. Everything in life will happen TO you rather than BECAUSE of you.

One major wrinkle in life I have often come across is the person who says they want to be married and does little to nothing about making themselves available to meet anyone. There may be nothing off-putting about them, but they act as if they will meet someone in their apartment or house because that is where they are every day after work. If their actions could speak, they would say, "I don't want to be with someone more than I want to be comfy at home every day." Maybe the actions would say, "I don't want to be with someone more than I want to watch eight straight hours of college football each Saturday ... unless it's March, then it is basketball." Or what about the traditionalist that would rather stick to her guns about being pursued than to take a risk and ask a guy out and maybe actually have a date? So many times our actions reveal our dishonesty with ourselves. It's hard, I know. We all do it in some way, shape, or form. Change happens when we are struck hard enough by the duplicity of our thoughts and actions.

The Declaration of Independence so eloquently states that we each have certain unalienable rights such as, "Life, liberty, and the pursuit of happiness." That document was written a long time ago by several of America's founding leaders. I have never seen the original text, but I learned about it from all of my teachers throughout my years in school. Imagine if I had never been exposed to what this piece of history endowed me with? What if I didn't know those were my rights? I would probably never question anything that threatened what the Declaration of Independence granted me. I might not ever operate with the full strength or capacity possible because I was not familiar with my rights. The same is true of your values!

> **Knowing what you want gives you freedom to pursue it**

Knowing what you want, being able to articulate it and see it vividly gives you the freedom and focus to pursue it. The stronger your connection is to your values, the greater the impact you will have. Knowing what you want gives you freedom to pursue it.

Chapter Four

4

THE NEED FOR CONNECTION

• •

Life is a series of moments all strung together. Like a web, these strings connect us to others around us. Shared events and experiences strengthen those bonds and connections. The same is true for the severing and disconnection of those bonds. As humans we have an innate need for a secure connection or attachment. There need not be a multitude of attachments, but at least one that is meaningful. These attachments are integral to our sense of belonging—our sense of knowing and being known. Family is often the primary source of these attachments, and probably the most complicated category of your personal life.

I love words. Understanding the layers of meanings for words is interesting to me, so I often look up definitions online, even for common words. One that made me laugh was the Urban

Dictionary's definition of family: "A bunch of people who hate each other and eat dinner together." No doubt family can be some of the most polarizing people on the planet. These are the folks who can annoy you, get on your very last nerve ... yet, you would do anything for them. Because of the complex, dimensional aspects of these familial relationships, it is important to know where you stand amidst the ebb and flow of life events. I distinguish family in two categories, immediate and extended. Immediate family is inclusive of the people you live with (or once lived with) in the same house: your spouse, children, parents, and siblings. If you had a unique experience that varies from this example, feel free to adapt its framework to your situation.

Parents or parental figures daily modeled their set of values for their children, whether they were aware of it or not. Most of us have built our values around what we experienced in our childhood homes. If we saw or experienced something we liked, we integrated it into our value system. If we saw or experienced something we didn't like, we excluded it ... and anything that resembled it, smelled like it, or may lead to it. The older, I mean, more experienced I become (as a parent myself), the more I realize that parents are just slightly older kids. When you're young, parents seem so serious and old. Now, as a parent myself, I can verify that most parents very much embrace their younger side after their children go to bed. Which is what we thought all along, right? It's why we came up

> **Most of us have built our values around what we experienced in our childhood**

with every possible reason to get out of bed—to prove that fun things were going on without us.

Most of us can pinpoint when we became parents, but few of us can determine when exactly we became adults. Adulthood does not automatically overtake you at a certain age or stage of life. This ambiguity explains why some adults have (and others have not) thought through the "whys" of what they do and don't do. Therefore, they go about doing things robotically, omitting things unintentionally that maybe they would do differently if they took some time and figured out their values. Not too long after our parents transitioned into adulthood, they had us to look after. Then as we, their children, subtly transitioned into adulthood, we found ourselves doing things without explanation, on autopilot. It isn't until someone comes along who does things differently, and challenges us in that area, that we evaluate whether we actually like our system or not.

Sibling rivalry is a real occurrence. Competition and comparison make sibling relationships among the most difficult, yet most valuable. The degree of commonality and shared experiences with them is like no other relationship on earth. Under normal circumstances you spend most of your childhood years in the company of your siblings—they are a huge shaping force in your confidence, esteem, and responses to life. Everyone compares you to your siblings—your parents, aunts and uncles, grandparents, teachers, coaches … everyone! Who is the smartest? The most photogenic? The funniest? The best athlete? The rule follower? The black sheep? The most successful? The most educated? The first to get married? The first to have children? The first to claim the favorite family name for the name of their child? Who is the one who makes mom and dad the most proud? ... the comparisons are endless.

Though my sisters and I are drastically different, there are a few common threads that run through us all. One of the things I was hung up on for many years was that the sister directly after me was and has always been the "skinny blonde one." I mean, where does she get off being so different from the rest of us? Growing up, she got more attention from boys, she got to wear the cute clothes, and she didn't have to work very hard to stay thin. No fair! Misdeal, reshuffle the cards please. It bothered me that we had the same parents, yet way different results in the metabolism department. I compared myself to her and felt like a failure. It wasn't until I was probably twenty or so that I was able to appreciate our differences rather than use them as a measuring stick. As I look at each of my sisters and how we were raised in the same home I am amazed at how different our value orders are. It makes me really proud of my parents and how they let us be ourselves.

One of the challenges that most siblings are not immune to is varying parenting styles. As I write this book, two of my three sisters and I have children. We all wanted to have children, and based on our interpretation of our upbringing and our current value system, we are raising our children the same and differently. At the end of the day, we each want to provide an ideal experience for our children and family. The means by which we get there in some cases is drastically different. I can't speak for my sisters on what their value order is on what they want to provide for their children but their actions are telling. Some of the things my sisters and their husbands are investing time, money, and energy into are themselves and their children having a strong education to position them for success, physically healthy habits, and concern for the welfare of animals. Some are not particularly religious but have causes they endorse. One facet of each of our parenting styles about which we differ is discipline. What one set of parents sees as permissible and acceptable, others do not agree. What one set views as appropriate consequences, the other might see as extreme. It can definitely make holidays and family reunions interesting!

As the eldest, I have had the most time to make mistakes and learn from them. I often thought this more extensive experience made it my duty to share my opinions. I have never been short on opinions. In my younger years, I assumed everyone wanted to know my opinion because it was awesome and always right. This was not the case with my sisters most of the time ... especially when it came to parenting strategy. But no matter our differences, I can say without doubt that at the core of our varying parenting tactics, we love our children and want the best for them. In that, we are united.

Children are the last portion of the immediate family group. They come along and shake everything up. What was valued even the night before the first child was born, is now subject to parental scrutiny once they arrive. For the child-enthusiasts, baby-proofing for safety becomes the ultimate sport. Time spent doing much else besides cuddling the little bundle becomes superfluous. You quickly become an expert in children's programing, spit-up predicting, diaper changing, and dreaming of their budding future. As they grow and become more expensive, opinionated and hormonal, it is important to anchor to your values as the children will do their best to stretch you.

Family is important and can be among the closest and most significant relationships you will ever experience. But not everyone has a "Leave it to Beaver" unit. Dysfunction is the functional reality for most of us. As we go through life, we develop intimate relationships with people outside the family gene pool, but every bit as close or closer. I like to think of these as the family we get to choose—our "Framily." Generally, they are people who are a little more like-minded to us, contributing to the time spent together being rather enjoyable. These relationships contribute greatly to our filters and the forming of our value order. Some of these close relationships cause us to grow and bring out the best in us, while others encourage bad habits and neglect. Our trajectory in life is greatly influenced by this group of people, which is why it is important to select them wisely.

Family and framily both play a huge role in the framework of our value order. Where we rank them determines a large part of the structure of our values. Is it at the center of our order or does it radiate from something else? Its position will have a huge bearing on where everything else comes into play. There is a good chance that where it is in our order has a lot to do with our foundational experiences. Some of us have had positive relationships with them and some of us have been devastated by them.

> **Family and "framily" both play a huge role in the framework of our value order**

FOUNDATIONAL EXPERIENCES SHAPE FUTURES

Life experience is a honing tool which shapes and sharpens our values. Some of us must have our own experiences and some can use the experiences of others to shape our values. The foundational experiences of childhood made the first impressions on our values. Remember my sixth grade graduation? It had a lasting impression and defined several of my values early on. Some of what we experienced as children, we choose to duplicate consciously and intentionally. Some is duplicated unintentionally and subconsciously. The last response to our childhood experience is that we do the opposite of what was done because the effects were undesirable to us.

Ted grew up in a home where his stepmom didn't work outside of the home (or inside) despite the fact that there were five children and two adults in the family. This caused Ted's father to have to work three or more jobs at one time just to support them, and for the children to have to grow up too quickly and take on the adult responsibilities for things like cooking and cleaning. Ted's father working all the time meant that he wasn't able to be around as much as any of them would have liked, but more importantly, needed. As a result, one of the main character qualities Ted looked for in a spouse was a strong work ethic. He wanted a woman who had been on her own for a bit, who had paid her bills, kept an apartment, held a job, and knew the value of a dollar. Ted knew for himself that if he was going to be married, he wanted a partner not a leach. He valued being part of a team where his wife contributed to the family, which then meant that he could be present with her and the children rather than largely absent from the home and exhausted when he was home. He did not value marriage for the sake of being married to just anyone more than contently single. He carefully and soberly selected someone who would support a strong family value.

My father and mother's marriage lasted 25 years, but then ultimately ended in divorce. There were flaws on both sides, but the straw that broke the camel's back was my dad's sexual orientation. How could he be married to my mom for this long all the while wanting something different? How could he be in our house every day and yet we did not see the truth? Who benefited from him keeping his lifestyle a secret? This deception caused me to not trust many men in my life—especially those in leadership roles. I didn't even know if I wanted to be married ... certainly not if this kind of thing could happen to me. I was not one of those ladies who had every detail of their wedding planned out before I met the groom. It seemed like a pointless venture if I wasn't ever going to get married. But despite the fact that I had no ceremonial preferences, I did know a thing or two about what kind of man it would take to get me to say yes.

One of the number one values I looked for in a spouse was straightforward honesty. I didn't need a man with a fancy job title, impressive income, or anything like that. I needed a man who was honest. The day that Ted and I met was Sunday, September 2, 2001. We were at a huge church in Grapevine, TX (a suburb of the Dallas/Ft. Worth area) in a singles class of around 500 people. I had attended there for several years post college, but hadn't met anyone that I saw as a potential match for me. A lot of the guys that went there seemed insecure in themselves, so to compensate for their feelings, they would inflate what they did or their status by making it out to be more impressive than it actually was. When I asked Ted what he did, his answer was that he delivered pizza for Domino's. What a refreshing response! If I asked any other guy whose job was to deliver pizza what they did, their answer would sound like, "I am a courier for a fortune 500 national company, in charge of customer satisfaction and time-sensitive job execution for each customer." While it may still be the truth, it is inflated and presumptuous. I valued being with someone honest more than with someone rich or impressive on paper. You can see how the framework of my family dynamic set the stage for me to place a high value on honesty.

An example of a value Ted and I saw growing up that we eventually wanted to duplicate, was the value of siblings. Before we had any children, we first weren't sure we could have them, second they were a lot of work and expense, and lastly we initially didn't want to be outnumbered by them because there could be mutiny! Alas, our first child Luke came. Luke was an absolute joy. He made us look like professional parents. He slept through the night by 6-7 weeks, no spit-up, gregarious and flexible. We were hooked. This kid thing was awesome! One Saturday morning around 8:45 a.m. about a year and a half later, Luke was still asleep and Ted and I were in bed relaxing. It dawned on me that we were getting an awful lot of sleep, therefore it could be time for another baby. He agreed, so open season began. Months and months passed and no signs of a baby. Around month nine, we decide to stop trying and focus on other things. At the one year mark, we found ourselves pregnant with our second child. I knew there would be work involved with this one as it took so long to get pregnant. We were invested, you know what I mean?

Little Kate made her entrance into the world and we had a pretty good scenario. One older boy to protect the younger sister. It looked good on paper. The first night home from the hospital, Kate cried the ENTIRE night! Had we made a mistake? What changed? Our home was so peaceful before. Four months later we find out she had a food allergy, got that remedied and all was well. She was a joyful, social baby. I could dress her up like a doll and she would cooperate. We decided we would keep her (wink). Things were very fun once she became a little mobile. Luke was ready for her to be a playmate. Seeing them play together must have made my ovaries twirl because when she was nine months old, we were SURPRISED to find out that number three was on the way. Another girl! Natalie was born and Kate turned into a little mother. Fast forward several years and our final child, Presley completed the family and the trifecta of daughters. These little people changed my world forever, forced me to become clear about my value order, and it is for our children that I write this book.

WHAT SHAPED YOUR VALUES?

What do you remember about what your parents valued? Here are some questions, some are funny some are serious, about how your parents do/did things. Take a minute or two to really think back and reflect on what was modeled for you. I would even say to write down the answers in a column.

- Were Mom and Dad around?

- Did they love each other? How did I know this?

- Did they love me? Why did I believe that?
- Did I feel safe in my home?
- Was there enough to eat?
- Did my mother stay at home with the children or work outside the home?
- What did my parents model? Did they emphasize education, sports, religion, community service, politics, pets, exercise, joy, anger, cleanliness, togetherness, independence, travel, rest, busyness, family, military etc.?
- What do I remember them sacrificing for? What was important enough to alter choices intentionally?
- What did they get excited about?
- What were their rituals or traditions when I was young?
- What was their work ethic like?
- Do I want to be like them?
- What do I swear I will never do that they did?
- How do they make me feel?
- How do they make others feel?
- Did they marry? For love? For security?
- Did they stay married or divorce somewhere along the way?
- Did they prepare me to launch out of the house?

- Did they set me up to always need them?
- What money habits did I learn from them?
- Do those habits help or hurt me now?
- Do I wish they would have been more open with me?
- Were they too open? Do I wish they wouldn't have shared so much with me as a kid?
- Did I feel safe?
- Did they make sure I got a good education?
- Did they make life too easy for me or just the right balance between "support" and "work for it"?
- What were their health habits?
- Were they friendly?
- Did they encourage us to believe in Santa Clause, or did they teach us Santa was a myth from the start?
- Did they feed us white bread or wheat?
- Were they night owls or early risers?

Make a second column directly across from the first. Note which of the answers are something you do the same or something you do differently. Lastly, make a third column. This column is the most important one for this exercise. This is where you write WHY you do things the same or WHY you do them differently. These reasons will help you identify some of your core values.

TO SANTA OR NOT TO SANTA?

I will give you an example from our family. The Santa element of Christmas is one that we elected not to include for our children. We each grew up in homes that did this differently (no Santa in my house, and Ted's house did Santa), but we both came to the same conclusion based on our experiences. My "why" for continuing the tradition of not including Santa was that my parents: 1) told us the truth, and 2) they got credit for all the work and purchasing that went into the presents they got us. For Ted, the Christmas when he was around nine years old was when things regarding Santa drastically changed. He recalls telling his dad that he wanted Santa to bring him some toy and shortly after asking, his dad told him to come to the garage with him. He went on to say something along the lines of, "Hey buddy, just want to make sure you know that Santa isn't the one doing the gifts and such. We get them all and that whole Santa thing isn't real."

Whenever Ted tells this story to me, even as a 40-year-old man, it is painfully obvious how this impacted him. He said, "It was then that I realized that my parents could lie to me, for years, without me knowing." Our wanting our children to know they can always trust us and them knowing where the gifts truly come from supersede the magic and wonder of a fictional character. Our values guided the decision on whether or not we included Santa in our Christmas experience.

When Luke, our oldest, was around six years old, he brought up something about Santa and I clarified to him that Santa wasn't real and that family members were where presents came from. Rather than believe me, he insisted that Santa was real because of the movie "Elf." As much as I did my part in following our family values, Luke wasn't ready to hear that particular truth. This can and will happen in your journey to living your values. You will have things that you believe in to your core, but it is up to those around you, including your children, whether or not they align themselves with them or not.

THE BEAUTY OF THE BEND

Have you ever noticed that palm trees are able to survive most of the hurricanes and storms that come through? Several factors are involved in their success but the one I want to focus on is their flexibility. They are not rigid like the Oak or Maple. The palm tree can bend nearly to the ground and bounce back once the storm ends. The palm tree isn't any less of a palm tree while it is adjusting to its stormy circumstances. It is doing what it must do to survive the storm and come back stronger. It chooses bending rather than breaking when things get difficult.

We all have heard the phrase, "The straw that broke the camel's back." This phrase doesn't mean there was only one straw, rather it was the one that made the load of straws it was already carrying finally too much now to bear. Our flexibility can be measured in straws or chances we give people or circumstances before we snap. The fewer the straws, the less flexible. The greater the straws, the more flexible. One of the most important factors determining our straw count is fatigue. I will talk more about the importance of rest later in the book, but it is worth mentioning here. When we are functioning on less than optimal sleep our ability to let certain things go greatly diminishes. Another factor is hunger. If you are hungry, or "hangry," which is how my family gets, and your children, or mother-in-law, or spouse does something that provokes you, your fuse is shortened because of the amount of messages your brain is trying to get to you to take care of the food problem. Their issue, which may not normally have gotten you so upset, has now caused you to make a full blown scene out of it and yourself.

One of my allocating times for this writing this book was when I was flying home from Texas by myself. My husband and father-in-law drove our kids back so that I would have several hours to write without much distraction. This particular trip home was following a long week visiting family all over the outskirts of the Dallas/Fort Worth area. Needless to say, I was pretty tired. I was psyching myself into writing mode despite my current energy level and it was around then that the first flight delay announcement came over the loud speaker. I notified my ride that I would be in a little bit late, but it shouldn't be too bad. The second delay announcement soon followed with another hour added to it. Anyone who wasn't ready to be flexible, quickly identified themselves.

They began expressing and exposing their lack of grace for the situation. The cause for the delay was weather related. The airline valued the safety of its staff and passengers and moved flights around to protect the very ones who were complaining. The desk representatives were forced to face numerous unhappy customers who were not satisfied with the safety reasons given to them. The lobby was filled with literally hundreds of people with varying levels of flexibility and understanding and acceptance of the situation. We were not going to get home now until well after midnight. Even as we boarded the plane over two and a half hours late, the ramp to the plane echoed with complaints and dissatisfaction regarding the airline. Although there were plenty of times I wanted to interject how ignorant those complaints were, I focused on the fact that the pilots and flight crew were going to be working the next two plus hours serving the less than thrilled passengers while I got to sit, rest, and write. Then I thought of the ground crew greeting us in Nashville and how it is likely to be after their shift would have been over if we had arrived on time and I was even more thankful to just get to be a passenger. I am usually at my worst when I am not being flexible. Can you relate?

The more you value someone, the more flexibility or grace you can offer them. This is ever so important with close relationships like that of a spouse. I can attest that one of the things I appreciate most about my husband is how flexible he is with me. He has allowed me to grow, change, try new things, pick up hobbies, put down hobbies, change my hair color, rearrange the furniture, change paint colors, reorganize the pantry, say we're having a garage sale and then put it off for weeks and weeks. He believes in me and knows that the path to success and fulfillment is a winding road most times. The years we have been together have been bathed in grace. Some years had more than others but overall we gave each other room to try things.

> **The more you value someone, the more flexibility or grace you can offer them**

I didn't start out being the most flexible of wives. I was a bit of a neat freak who enjoyed the bed getting made every morning and was able to relax just after all the flat surfaces were cleaned at night. Ted questioned me about the bed making saying we would be getting right back into in that night and he didn't usually see the dirt or clutter on the countertops at all at that time. He didn't care about the cleanliness of our one bedroom apartment but he did care about me.

TIME TO GO

One of the easiest ways to understand how individuals stay in negative relationships or family situations is that those relationships often represent the only attachment felt by that person. They view it, most basically, as even a bad relationship is better than none. Those with the damaged connections must weigh out the cost of continuing the relationship, possibly subjecting themselves to further damage, but also the possibility of healing and reconciliation. We want to believe that people can change and become better human beings—especially when it pertains to those closest to us.

Reestablishing connection to a damaged or even challenged relationship with healthy boundaries is something that can be done on your part if it is within your value order. One example of this for me was when I was transitioning into college years. I am the oldest of four girls and my younger sisters and I were all born within six years. Talk about wild times! There is not a mild personality among the bunch either. As it was getting closer to the time I was to go away to college, my sisters became increasingly annoying. I thought something was wrong with our family because we were fighting so much. I had friends who had such beautiful relationships with their siblings that it made me jealous. I admit those dynamics weren't exactly apples for apples, but they still were appealing. Fall came and I moved out of the house and into the dorm four hours away. Ahhhhhhh. Space. My first visit home was probably the most enjoyable time with my sisters I had ever had up until that moment. We could actually really appreciate each other because of having had some time apart. The saying about distance making the heart grow fonder rang true for me more than ever. Of course, like any opportunistic younger sisters, they raided my makeup and closet while I was away at school, so as soon as I realized it and reclaimed my things it was time to go back to school so I could like them again. (With a barricade in place to guard my things while I was away again!)

This is a silly and pretty common example, but the truth of doing what is necessary to better the connection is there. I valued the relationships, and to improve its condition at that time, it required time apart and time together … and a barricade!

Some relationships we value are currently toxic. Sometimes it's circumstances beyond our control causing the stress on a relationship. Life altering illness, change in marital status, job loss, birth of a child, death of a loved one, financial trouble, relocation, extraordinary success, and many more circumstances can change a relationship temporarily and possibly even permanently. When these events occur, they demand something of both parties involved. The more valuable the relationship, the more flexible you will want to be to preserve the connection. Imagine that palm tree I mentioned earlier. When pressure is placed on it externally, it will best survive if it is flexible. The rigid trees will likely be damaged and potentially snap.

A few years ago, one of my good friends, a high value friend, always had a lot going on. She had multiple children, her own business, and a husband whose work placed a great deal of demand on him. Countless times over the years, we would make plans to hang out or to do stuff together with our kids. However, our percentage of plans accomplished was very low. Numerous things would come up that, for her, took precedence over our plan. The first ten to twenty times this happened, my feelings were hurt and I was disappointed that those "things" kept interfering. The plans that were cancelled were even more painful at that time because my husband was working part-time while he was a full-time nursing student. His time being nearly completely spoken for left me alone more than I really wanted to be, so anytime I had an activity scheduled, I really looked forward to it. I was desperate for adult/friend conversation and interaction. It would have been very easy for someone with my personality to get tired of the cancelled plans and walk away from the relationship because I couldn't depend on her.

What I eventually realized was that she was a friend who needed me to be flexible. Each time our plans got cancelled, I took it personally when I shouldn't have. It wasn't that she didn't want to hang out, rather it was that something higher on her value order required her attention and our time was the only optional time she had to spend on it. When we were able to spend time together, it was great. We both walked away feeling invested in and thankful that nothing came up. Another word for this flexibility is grace. We live in a very demanding culture where grace is nearly extinct. I think we all would be surprised at how far a little grace would go today.

KNOW WHEN TO WALK AWAY, KNOW WHEN TO RUN

There are times when a relationship has run its course or has become virulent. It is difficult when it is one with a family member or friend. The history, the rare occasion of a positive time together, or past good times no longer amount to enough to balance out the cost of damage being done. How are we to know when it's the right time to exit the relationship? Is it a permanent exit or a temporary one? In our family, there are individuals on both sides who have little to no involvement in our lives. Some I wish had more and some I am okay with it being limited. One person in particular left a huge wake every time they would pop back in to our lives and pop out. They would passive-aggressively imply that the relationship strain is due to our unsubstantiated judgments rather than their scorching case of narcissism.

This person would call bi-annually when it was convenient but not call when it was a birthday or anniversary. Important dates began going unmentioned and uncelebrated. This was not so hard to tolerate when it was just Ted and me, but once we had children and they were subjected to this on again, off again style of involvement, it became very hurtful. It reached a point that we decided that some course of action had to be taken. The least painful way for us was to simply be uninvolved and ambivalent back. It took the pressure off and we didn't have to be subjected to their fickle feelings about us and being a family.

For some, the abusive relationship leaves no option but to exit. Value you and your future enough to remove yourself and begin healing. What if it is simply a challenging relationship? Over the years, I have heard numerous people talk about a mother-in-law problem that sucked the air out of every holiday for them. Two of them were friends of mine who solved the dilemma the same way. It wasn't awesome, but it was a solution. They simply didn't go. As unfortunate as it was for the spouse and the children, it saved everyone the discomfort of the spectacle. The spouse and children went for a few days around the main holiday and returned to spend the main holiday at home. One thing that I want to stress here is the value of unity. If a person, especially an in-law, unduly lays into you in the presence of your spouse (who came from that Cruella De Vil woman, yet you love them still) it is imperative that the spouse stands with you and even defends you to them. Challenging people often have a divisive personality and love to see people left afloat by their mate. Keeping that front unified dampens any hot air they attempt to blow your way.

Value yourself enough to walk away from abusive relationships

Another relationship to edit is the one-way friendship. The mooch, the one who never calls to initiate, the one who never asks anything about you, the "Can I borrow everything and not return or repay ever?" type are ones to reroute out of your valuable time and energy. Don't waste your resources on people who don't see or appreciate your value. One of my former pastors used to say, "Be where you're celebrated, not just tolerated." The more guff you put up with, the lower you value what you have to offer this world. Knowing your value is just as important as knowing your value order. It will help you be more judicious with your time and energy.

Determining your value order in this category can be more challenging because there are nuances and variables involved as well as other people and their values. Your part in it all is determined by you and it has permission to change as life does. Do not feel responsible or entitled to change or control other people's values. This is often easier said than done. Our personal lives contain more choices that are subject to our value order preference than say our work lives, so it is easy to become a value campaigner. Remember, this process is about clarifying what you value not about convincing others to share your values.

CHAPTER FIVE

5

OFFICE SPACE

EMPLOYEE, MANAGER, OWNER

There are three main lenses to look through in the area of work: as an employee, as a manager, or as an owner. Each one has a different perspective or vantage point and different expectations. Knowing what you value and how to get what you want most out of your career are synergistic. Let's look first through the eyes of an employee. Gone is the golden age of a seven-hour workday with a long lunch, and a generous retirement plan. The majority of companies are expecting fewer people to do the work of many. Thus, most people are living to work versus working to live based on the amount of time they put into it. With the employer dictating the terms, what choices remain in your power to allow your career to align with your value order? How can you define your values under someone else's jurisdiction? It is important to understand how much you actually are in control of many features of your employment.

WORK ETHIC

First and foremost, you control your work ethic. Showing up ready to work and giving your best is an uncommon, highly noticeable character quality that speaks volumes without you having to say a word. In the past, when I have had the chance to interview applicants for a job opening, the ones with the most to say often were the ones with the worst work ethic. This does not mean you should be awkwardly silent or overly brief, but don't over-promise or over-sell. I love what one of my professors in college said when we asked him how long one of our papers should be. He said, "Your paper should be like a good skirt. Long enough to cover the subject, but short enough to keep it interesting." Job candidates who give confident, concise responses were most often the ones who subsequently gave the best job performance. It took me a little while to realize this. Impressive talkers can be convincing. But "getting in the door" is far different than remaining there without a fall from grace. Many eager, flash-in-the-pan talkers later, I figured it out. Seeing through the cloud of B.S. many people use as a smokescreen to hide their reality isn't usually worth it—too often what's behind that cloud is the same ... sh-tuff.

Let's assume you have a great work ethic, one that you are proud of. You have made yourself indispensable for the sake of job security. This might also make you irreplaceable, and therefore unable to be promoted because you are the only one who can figure out your elaborate filing system or super-secret coding scheme. Be replaceable. Work hard out of pride in what you are not out of fear of what you may lose. Be promotable. Leaders identify, educate, and train future leaders. If you are not currently a leader but would like to be, diligent work, efficiency, and timeliness mixed with a decent level of care for the company you work for, are a good place to start. Think of the times as a customer you have experienced an employee talking with another employee about how many hours are left in their shift or watching the clock for the last 40 minutes of their workday? Their presence on the job becomes a decrease in value for the company rather than an increase. I know that not every job is a dream job, but if you work like you own the company, you may encounter your promotion through a customer seeing and reporting your excellent job performance.

I give you the story of George C. Boldt. Boldt was an immigrant from Europe in 1864 who came to the U.S. with virtually no money. The only job he could procure was that of a dishwasher in a hotel. He tried a move to Texas in search of better employment, but was unable to find any so he returned to New York and took on yet another job in a hotel kitchen. He finally caught a break and moved up to cashier where his stellar work ethic and customer service standards caused the hotel's owner to take notice. It was not much later that he was promoted to hotel manager. A little while later, Boldt relocated to Philidelphia where he continued his journey in the hotel management business at the Bellevue hotel. One fateful night in Philadelphia, there was terrible weather and the Bellevue was full to capacity. A couple came in to see about a room and Boldt informed them of their lack of vacancy. However, Boldt being a man who modeled going above and beyond to take care of his customer, offered the couple his room at the hotel for the night. This act of kindness and superior work ethic spoke volumes to the husband and wife. The husband's name was William Waldorf Astor. Over the next two years, he and Boldt developed a friendship. At around the two year mark of their friendship, The Waldorf Hotel in New York City opened and at Astor's request, George C. Boldt was its manager. Boldt not only ran The Waldorf with excellence, he also had a large part in the mediation to join The Waldorf and The Astoria Hotels together under one umbrella called The Waldorf Astoria.

Boldt's journey from kitchen at a no name hotel to front desk at the most opulent hotel of its era, was not a fluke. It was not luck that made the impression on William Astor to keep in contact with a standout employee. Boldt knew that each dish he washed with excellence was a valuable stepping-stone to his future. Each customer he went above and beyond for was worth all the effort because it positioned him to be ready for promotion when the opportunity arose. Most of us value our incomes and appreciate the life choices they provide. Most of us would be thrilled to be promoted and have our incomes go up with that. However, what most of us are NOT doing is positioning ourselves for that promotion by going above and beyond where we are. I don't mean working more and more hours, but rather being more productive, by being a more valuable player in the workplace. We want the gold star for

> **Each task you perform with excellence is a valuable stepping stone to your future**

doing the things required of us in our job description. Fulfilling your job description is the least you should be doing if you want to move up and increase your workplace value.

If your current workplace doesn't flow with your value order, be proactive and search for a better fit. In the summer of 2010 after over eight years of employment, Ted decided he had had enough of working in a non-temperature controlled warehouse. He wasn't getting home until nearly 7 p.m. during the week. Saturdays were spent doing chores and yard work and Sundays were church followed by collapsing from the pace of the week only to get up on Monday and do it all over again. He was missing so much of our children's lives and only seeing them when they were exhausted and at their worst. He had really wanted to pursue nursing when we were first married, but we were not able to sustain ourselves without his income at the time. So in August of 2010, Ted and I reached beyond the threshold of patience with his job and agreed for Ted to leave it and enroll in nursing school full-time.

The end goal of Ted being a nurse was for our family to be able to be together more with him working three twelve-hour shifts per week. However, over the next four and a half years, we had to invest more time to reach that goal. I invested more time into working due to the fact that I shifted into the role of primary income provider. Ted got a wonderful part-time job and was enrolled in full-time school, which not only came with classes but HOMEWORK! Ted's workload for school was consuming. Our oldest, Luke, was steadily bothered by how unavailable his dad was for so long. We both had to continually remind him of our end goal. We had to establish the fact that this was all so that Daddy could have more time with him and his sisters once finished. This was a hard sell. Luke had his doubts because he had only experienced getting less of his dad's time. The same thing applies when I work on a book or a speaking experience. My end goal is always to have more time with my family.

In the area of career, there are several values to explore where they rank with you. Knowing this order will help you in the job and company selection. When you step into a job that is a better fit for you and your values it will increase your personal career satisfaction and fulfillment. It is important to remember that you are not the only one in the interview process. You also want to know as much as you can about the employer and the work environment so that you can make a wise decision for you. People often end up in jobs they don't like because they did no interviewing. Their mental position before going into the interview was, "I hope they pick me," rather than, "Is this going to be mutually beneficial?" or "Do I believe in this company and stand behind the way they treat their customers and employees?" Believe in yourself and your values enough to be judicious when selecting a job.

FLEXIBILITY

When seeking a job, I encourage you to underscore the flexibility of the company. This is often not examined enough by applicants. Life happens. How does this employer handle situations which require flexibility? Are they tyrannical, obliging, or overly permissive? Is it hard for you to watch people taking advantage of a soft boss by consistently drumming up excuses for tardiness or absence? If so, working for a boss like that may be a deal breaker. The root issue becomes a respect problem for your boss and that is a dangerous place to from which to work. If the manager likes to micro-manage every breath you take and doesn't validate a sick child or spouse as a reason you should miss work, then that could be a deal breaker. The root issues here become not only job related, but also family related. The spouse or child could begrudge the job and feel less valuable simply because of a management style that doesn't support your value order.

BENEFIT/COST

Income/Expense is the next value to take into consideration. Do you know what you need to bring home in order to support yourself and your family? Have you evaluated what it would cost to take that position? Will it require new clothes, dry cleaning, work boots, certifications or licenses? How far away is it? How long, with traffic, should commuting take you every day? For most of us more is more, however, there are times when more comes at a high cost. I have so many friends and colleagues who travel for work. Some enjoy and look forward to the travel and some do it only because it is a means to an end. The percentage of travel varies with each company and position, so it is critical for you to know how much that is worth to you. If you love to travel, then this is a bonus feature. If you prefer to be with family or friends in the evenings or free time, traveling in high percentages will conflict with your value order.

Value order conflicts are only sustainable in the short term. They wear on you over time and your life expectancy at a job with said conflicts is shortened NO MATTER the income. The lure of a higher income is hard for most to pass up despite the fact that it often is attached to a hook and a line. The prestige of climbing income brackets and ranks is something that makes going to high school reunions that much sweeter. I get it. I am not immune to the appeal of niceties, but I have to remind myself that even promotions are going to cost somewhere.

QUALITY OF THE COMPANY

Another item to evaluate is the company itself. Here are some questions that will help you determine if a company is a good fit for you.

- How does the company set up your growth and future with them?

- How is the work environment?

- Is everyone in cubicles? Will you have to share a cubicle?

- How does the management oversee their staff: from a distance, or right on top of them?

- Is your job performance and evaluation based on teamwork or individual work?

- Do they take the time to understand you and your personality and how you are best motivated and communicated with?

- Do they invest in furthering your training or education?

- If you are a creative person, does your position allow for creativity?

- Do you believe in the products or services offered by the company?

- Do you have a say in who your clients are?

- Do they have a good business model in place to ensure they are going to be around and able to sustain themselves?

If any of these areas conflict with your values, you may not experience maximum fulfillment in your job. These questions are not here to keep you from working, but rather to have you know exactly what you are entering into. Being informed and having correct expectations before starting a new job are priceless. The chances of experiencing the job that is described to you at the interview are few and far between. Job postings and descriptions are about as accurate as online dating profiles. Everyone wants to sound great to get you to apply and accept. It is worth doing due diligence to make sure the job is what it says it is and that other employees can corroborate what is being offered.

DON'T PANIC, PREPARE

Alas, if you are currently in a job that is not congruent with your value order, don't panic, prepare. Update and revise your resume and begin interviewing. I have a few friends who enjoy their jobs but make it a habit to interview for other jobs on a regular basis. When they first told me they did this I was confused as to why they did all of that extra work. "Options" was one of their responses. They wanted to know they always had options.

"Keeping [their] interview skills sharp," was another reason. But one of my favorite reasons was to see what employment and benefit packages other companies were offering. You interview differently when you are employed than when you are unemployed. Even if you are happy where you are, you may want to try doing one or two interviews every six months. It can be a good practice to introduce yourself to other companies and to interview them as well.

There will be seasons when the perfect job for you now isn't the perfect job for you in the next season. This is normal. It is rare to find a job that satisfies each season of your life without any alteration. The key to remaining in a job that aligns with your value order is to periodically evaluate your situation. If you feel like things are a good fit and really flowing well for you, identify what aspects are behind those feelings. The same is true if you are not happy at your job. One of the biggest categories I would like you to pay close attention to is if your job USED to be an ideal situation and has changed to one which you are ready to leave. This is where you have a huge opportunity to clarify your values if they were ever vague to you. Questions to ask yourself would be:

- What changed in my personal life?
- Did my relationship status change?
- Did I add a child to our family?
- Did we move to a new location?
- Is there something outside of my work environment that I wish I had time/availability to do?
- Did anyone in my family's health change?

These are a few to begin with for considering major changes in your personal life which affect job satisfaction. Questions regarding your job could be something like these:

- Did the management change?
- Did another employee I came into contact with regularly change or leave their position?
- Did my hours get cut?
- Did my hours get expanded?
- Did I get a raise that reflected my work ethic?
- Did I get the promotion I had hoped for?
- Now that I am a few years into this career, do I still like what I am doing or is it getting monotonous?
- Did they change my position into something outside my skills set making work frustrating?
- Are they trying to squeeze me out and get me to quit by micro-managing me or jacking with my schedule?

THE LENS OF A MANAGER

If you are in the position of manager then your lens filter will still encompass all the things we talked about for an employee, but you will also have to expand your lens to let your view be just a bit broader. Remember, honesty will always be the best policy as far as selecting the staff that will fill the needs of your department. Some questions you may include are:

- What areas are my weakest? How can I staff that weakness and concentrate more of my energy behind my strengths?

- Are the right people in the right positions on the right team? Consider personality profiling to make sure the area you are placing a new hire will be a good fit for them.

- What are the strengths and weaknesses of every employee under my charge? Who am I underutilizing? Who is taking advantage of their job?

- Is there anyone on my team who needs to be promoted or replaced?

- What kind of leader am I? Do I generate an atmosphere of trust and mutual respect?

Take the time to know what each employee under your leadership values and do your best to accommodate them knowing that happy employees perform best.

THE LENS OF AN OWNER

Finally, we get to the owner's lens and can explore the variations they must consider. When I had my small talent agency years ago, I had as few as one and as many as four employees at any given time. I am sure they can attest to the fact that I was not an awesome boss. I was the paranoid small business owner. I was constantly afraid I was being taken advantage of. Almost a decade later, I found out when I took the Myers-Briggs® personality test that the biggest fear of my personality type is "Being taken advantage of." It totally makes sense now, and

I wish I had known then that my feelings were predominantly internal.

I remember thinking to myself that I wanted people to enjoy their work experience, but not too much. I didn't mind people leaving work on time if I knew their day was productive. I wanted them to have time with their family, time to work out, time to separate from work, but most of all I wanted to know that they loved the company as much as I did and worked that way. I eventually got the memo that no one loved the company like I did and that was an unrealistic expectation.

Another type of owner is the absentee owner. I have worked for an owner like this before and it was very frustrating. They verbally communicated with me when I was hired, then once the dust settled, it was obvious they were gone. Even in the movies, this type of ownership is likely to have unfortunate consequences. Ownership generally communicates investment and value, but when the actions scream otherwise, it is difficult for anyone to want to get behind it. If you are thinking that one day you want to own a company and have no involvement, you had better make sure you have a manager with very strong convictions—otherwise your lack of involvement will likely sink the ship.

I have, at different times in my life, been around different employer styles that I never could gel with and I realize now it is because I have a different value system than them. When I first moved to Nashville, I met and was mentored by a very successful talent manager. One of the things he said to me early on was that he looked for those who came in early and stayed late as potentials to move up in his company. A giant buzzer went off (in my head that is) like a zonk or a whammy on those game shows that this would never be a place in which I would move up because I do not value my job more than time with my family. The fact that I recognized the ill fit early on saved me from a path that would have had little to no harmony with my core values. There were plenty of individuals lining up to work under this man and willing to sacrifice nearly everything to one day be in a place like he was. Yay for them. There are spouses in this world who are uniquely wired to be able to handle being married to people who love to work long hours. I am not one of those and neither is my husband, so we seek out careers that play into our value order well.

If you struggle finding an employment opportunity that lines up with your values, one avenue I strongly recommend is the self-employment option. Not everyone needs to be in a direct sales, multi-level marketing cosmetic, fitness supplement, vitamin, essential oil, cleaning product pushing situation. There are plenty of other things you can do as an entrepreneur. Things like landscape design, cleaning houses or businesses, childcare, personal trainer, therapist, stylist, personal chef, mobile auto detailer, writer, consultant … plus many, many more options. Each able to be set up with your values in mind. If you are interested in discovering what work you love to do, I suggest you get Dan Miller's book, *48 Days to the Work You Love*. This book helped Ted and many others narrow the field down to gain clarity at what careers could provide a great amount of fulfillment while providing a paycheck as well.

Harmony with what you do for work is one of the large pieces of the fulfillment puzzle. Remember, you spend the better part of your "awake hours" in this position week after week. Taking home some sense of gratification is the goal. It is healthy to desire a job that provides this because at the end of the day, you enter your personal life with whatever remaining energy you have. If you are in a job that you hate, it is an energy drain. The more fulfilling the job, the more energy it preserves for your personal life.

Harmony between your values and what you do for work is a large piece of the fulfillment puzzle

CHAPTER SIX

6

CENTERED SELF

PUT YOUR MASK ON FIRST

Without our health, none of our values are possible. Being healthy, getting healthy, or becoming healthier are all positive goals and help facilitate us reaching more and more of our potential. There are many facets of our health to look at when evaluating our value order. Physical fitness, mental fitness, emotional wellness, physical wellness, diet, and our vices are a few that have a broad scope. Does the way you take care of yourself underscore your values? If one of your values is to be able to play with your children or grandchildren, are you taking the daily steps to make that happen? If one of your values is to quit smoking once and for all, are you finding ways to reduce your stress, thus reducing the urge to need that cigarette? Our body is the only vehicle we have to live out our values. It makes sense to give it what it needs to produce energy.

Everything we value requires our energy, which has a limited supply and varying quality. We often go into the most challenging of times with the lowest supply and quality of energy because of what predicated the challenge. A prime example of this would have to be the holidays. The weeks preceding Thanksgiving and Christmas are when work has to be done ahead of time at double speed, travel plans must be made, school-aged children have exams, projects, and papers due. Don't forget you have to get the awkward Secret Santa gifts for the co-worker you hardly know and the cupcakes you have to bring to your child's class free of all allergens. Then there is packing for you and yours, leaving your house clean-ish, taking the dog to the pet sitter, remembering to bring all the gifts you know will end up in the trash in less than a week ... and the list goes on. I'm sure there is more to your story as there is to mine, but you get the idea. We go from this hectic, crazy and exhausted pre-game show at our own home then cram family and extended family into the designated house where a good bit of nostalgia (both positive and negative) gets re-hashed, and you hope for the best over the next week. When you spell it all out like that, you can see it can easily spell disaster. Ours is particularly fun because we have nearly every political party represented and a Baskin Robins' style variety on religion as well. Just dandy.

A friend of mine once said, "Remember to put your mask on first." I didn't quite catch the reference at first, but then I remembered every time I travel by plane with one of my children, the flight attendant reminds me to put my mask on first and then assist those who would need my help. This illustration is critical to understanding the difference between being in the space of centered self and not self-centered. To have the greatest impact, we must have the wisdom to provide ourselves with the necessary things that produce our best physical and emotional behavior. For example, I can tell when my children are tired. Silly things upset them, they make poor choices that then require some form of discipline, which then results in more crying. The best thing for me to do as their parent would be to get them to bed as soon as possible. This will greatly reduce the discipline issues as well as get them what they truly need in that moment despite all of their denial.

Another facet of putting your mask on first would be to incorporate time for what your personality needs. If you are more of an introvert, build in time to pull away and be alone in your thoughts. If you are an extrovert, set up a friends' night or get-together and recharge. If hitting the gym or track gets you less crunchy, then by all means just do it.

One of the most repetitive challenging experiences for me is the daily dinner to bedtime circus. Everyone in the house is pretty much spent, dinner has yet to be prepped or cooked, ninja-like children forage for the quietest snack they can attain without my noticing and the beloved "Babe, what's for dinner?" question hits that nerve that puts me straight into crazy town. Ted or I will then make whatever dinner was on the docket, or settle for the item in the front and center of the freezer. We place the food in front of the children and see if we can actually make it to our seat before the complaints or "concerns" begin about the meal. With each negative statement my energy drops further and my patience wanes. This is no Norman Rockwell portrait going on here. Where did I go wrong?

The evening progresses into the bedtime struggle until the last bit of crying has stopped and there is peace and quiet. Clean up ensues with a side of grown-up conversation usually finishing up the last drops of energy that I had. I need to refuel. For me, one of the most effective things is quality time with my husband. I will get a second wind just by sitting down with him and debriefing about our day, high/low, funny things and then I am in a head space to actually sleep versus worrying all night. If I don't get that time with him, the deficit trickles into the next day. I also have the need for a few close friends. I am energized by sincere, funny, down-to-earth people, especially if they are quick witted and can layer a joke well. Many times after being around someone like that, Ted will say that I am on a "life high" which is always fun.

I know my personality well enough to know that I need to be near people and this is a value to me. How this value is honored is in things such as where our homes have been located. I function best being near our friends, church, retail and grocery stores, and the YMCA. Living far from these things could potentially have a negative impact resulting in my not being able to function in my fullest capacity. I put my mask on first when it comes to where I locate my family because my husband is mostly introverted and doesn't have that same need.

Then there is the ever popular "Me Time." This phenomenon has grown by leaps and bounds with the prevalence of homes having to be dual income. It has gotten out of control for some because of its self-centered mentality. May I suggest that you evaluate those things which are categorically "Me Time" activities and run it through the filter of how does this affect my family, my friendships, and my finances? If these things truly replenish you and allow you to make the time when you return and re-engage with your family better quality, then they are worthwhile. If they underscore deficiencies you feel you have to endure or leave you feeling like you "deserve" them because of all the hardships you face as a responsible adult, exercise caution. Feeding this need will leave you unfulfilled, and turn your focus inward. Make sure the things you do to replenish you are in harmony with all of your other values.

TABLE TALK

Car time is one of my least favorite times. I struggle with any activity or commitment that requires a long drive. I value being in proximity to as many things as possible, which frees me to not spend so much of my own and my family's time in the car. My husband and I place a high value on our time together and our time as a family (even the crazy parts) which influences our decisions on what we will and will not be part of. One of our top values in the category of family time is meal time. As much as possible, this time together occurs at the table. I love when all six of us eat together and we get to hear about the "World according to Natalie" report, or see the latest magic trick Luke has learned involving the salt shaker. In our culture, it is popular and almost noble to be so on the go with your schedule and your children's schedule that you only have time to eat fast food in the car every night of the week. Swimming, football, dance, cheer, yoga, small group, bunko, volunteering ... all good things when done in moderation or balance. However, most people over-commit themselves and their families and reduce meal time to some chicken nuggets and fries phenomenon shoved in between karate and little league. Everyone is tired. The kids are exhausted, mom and dad are officially chauffeurs, the siblings hardly know each other, and the dream of everyone having time to sit around a table for a healthy home-cooked meal is only for underachievers. Holding fast to a standard for a certain number of meals to be had at home, at the table, all together promotes many more values than one more activity will ever return. These meals are where some of the best memories are made.

Another benefit of being hospitable and spending time around the table is that the quality of the food is generally better for you. You have more control or at least awareness of how much salt, butter, oil and sugar has gone into what you are eating. This is good for everyone involved!

On the flip side of family dinner is the life of the single person. If you find yourself in this category and your dinners are always the frostbitten cuisine meals or fast food in the car, then it may be time to increase the frequency you dine with other people. Invite them over, cook for them (or at least pick it up at the local grocer's deli), and make memories. You have stuff worth sharing. Jokes, experience, perspective, even a listening ear are all things that you can offer them and theirs in return. There is a huge lost art called hospitality that if left unnoticed, may go into extinction. Hospitality is defined as the "friendly and generous reception and entertainment of friends and guests." For many, this is something quite foreign. We only know going out to eat anymore. "What if I don't have the space in my home or cooking skills? What if my house is a mess?" The good news is that you don't have to wait until your house is perfectly clean to invite them over. Focus on the few rooms you will be in and that's all folks. And while I am on the topic of hospitality and values, put your phone down! Be where you are. Listen to what is happening in the room there with you and don't worry what anyone else is doing. Ted and I have begun eliminating time we spend with people who can't leave their phone alone while we are hanging out with them. It translates rude and conveys an attitude of lack of appreciation for what it is costing us to be with them. Be mindful that time is the most valuable gift we can give to anyone. So when someone is giving it to you, take care to be present.

A MOMENT OF AUTHENTICITY

Health is one of the ultimate values we should all share. This is a hard one because it based largely on a series of small, seemingly inconsequential decisions. To be completely transparent, this is an area I struggle with. I have never been a small person and have had varying levels of guilt and shame as a result. In my mind I know that I should be different and should be able to will to weigh less, but it hasn't happened like that for me yet. I see people all around me in the same struggle and every once in a while someone changes and stays changed. I appreciate the dedication and decision management those individuals have. It encourages me that it can be done. Being healthy (which would translate for me to weigh less) at this point is an ideal. Ideal means "existing only in the imagination, desirable or perfect but not likely to become a reality." Ideals are things we love to talk about. Talking about them actually satisfies our brain the same way as physically doing them. An ideal is an area where what we think we value is not what we choose to value or act upon all of the time. Remember when I spoke about the gap between what we want and what we experience? Ideals are usually one of the main culprits. Nothing changes if all we do is think about what we think we should be like.

I openly share my struggle with you to let you know that even though I have written this book and I do have some areas pretty together, there is still room for improvement. Like me, you may find you truly do have some things in order, but other areas that still require work. Defining and walking out your values is a journey. When you are doing better, remind yourself that better is better. Each choice is like putting a penny in the penny jar or removing a penny. They all have an impact over time. Forward momentum is felt when a bunch of pennies are put in the jar in a row. You can begin to see the increase, feel the success, and be encouraged to go further once you not only start depositing into the things you truly value, but continue depositing consistently.

> **Defining and walking out your values is a journey**

This is an important time to reflect on the possible diversion between what you think you value and what you demonstrate that you actually value. Remember, the goal here is to close the gap or chasm between what we value and what we experience. Try this: On the back of a business card, draw a "+" and a "-" with a line separating the two. For each better choice you make, no matter how small, give yourself a hashmark in the "+" column. The same goes for not so good choices. It will help you see in a day or two where your values lie. Remember, better is better. It may be that you need to incorporate yourself into an exercise group or something to get you into better physical health and that is where doing it alone has failed you. It may be that you find a food journal buddy or a nutritionist. It may be that you begin with one small change and see it add up like walking for 15 minutes a day, every day, no excuses. You will feel the momentum shift and your mind will get in line.

SABBATH, NOT SELFISH

We were not designed to run 24 hours a day, 7 days a week all year long. Our bodies regenerate on rest. Our efficiency, creativity, physical performance, mental performance, and emotional balance all improve with rest. Yet we deny ourselves this rest in the name of success, children's activities, money, promotion, the dangling carrot of retirement, a bigger television, new purse, new phone, more miles clocked, volunteer hours, and many more. This self-destructive pace is something we would complain about if our mom, dad, or child were doing it, but when we are the ones doing it we have every excuse to drive ourselves into the ground. One of the Ten Commandments directs us to take a Sabbath day or rest day once a week. It doesn't have to be on Saturday or Sunday exclusively, but it does need to be intentionally protected. If rest is on God's Top Ten List don't you think it is something worth honoring in our own lives? "In our culture, work has become a god. It is the pre-eminent factor in organizing human life and establishing personal identities. It so dominates people's lives that there is little time for themselves or their families... [The Sabbath] is designed to protect us from the dangers of physical exhaustion, psychological stress, and the interpersonal alienation which result from idolization and over-identification with work."1 Add to work the fact that we try to be involved in everything stemming from a deep rooted fear-of-missing-out or being less popular. What happens is that in each of those things we participate in, they are getting low quality energy because we took little to no time to rest.

Resting is not the same thing as sleeping. Rest is to "stop engaging in strenuous or stressful work in order to relax." Rest for some may be a walk outside or it may be reading a book inside. The biblical Sabbath had much more depth than just the physical aspect. I had the privilege of going to Israel for nine days back in 2011. The trip was fantastic. I was able to go while my husband and children were in school at the time and just be responsible for me. We toured the country, seeing many beautiful, historical sites as well as observing the diverse culture there. Once Saturday came, all Jewish portions of the country shut down. They were all in their homes or at the beach surrounded by their family and friends. No one dared work on the Sabbath but more importantly, no one wanted to work on the Sabbath. The expectation of the community was that Friday was the day to get all business completed for the weekend and that no businesses would be open to serve the public on Saturday. I admit, I was jealous of their culture in that moment. I also was convicted in my own life about thinking I was above one of the commandments. I justified it for years because of Ted's college or the children, but really it was a choice I was making to not make it happen. Most of us know of a few businesses that actually shut down for a day or so a week. For example, we know that Chik-fil-A will not be serving up their delicious chicken sandwiches on Sundays because they honor the fact that people need time away from work including managers. I am never impressed when someone says they work 60-80 hours a week. In fact, I think the opposite, which is the fact that they have to make up for low quality work with more hours OR that they didn't have a voice to stand up for their value of time away from work to regenerate and renew for a better quality the next day. Certainly there are busy seasons, but the chronic overtime workers are simply not rested and not achieving balance.

The good news is that balance is becoming more and more popular as people are realizing how tired they are of the pace at which their lives are going. They have a thousand pictures of little Johnny or Emma playing sports but very little conversational substance. They have money in the bank but no time to spend it. They have personal days to take but no one to take them with. These predicaments come from a poor dispersal of time due to a disconnection from our values. We see how others divide up their time and feel pressure to do the same because we have not established our own identity, our belief, our value, our why!

Take the time to connect to your why. Your value order is not simply an ideal order. It is a statement of how you will live your life, what to keep, what to release, what to begin, and what to end. It is unique to you and will have the most power when it is abided by. At the end of the day you can lay your head on the pillow guilt-free and satisfaction-filled knowing that you remained true to you. That feeling of homeostasis and authenticity is energizing and centering. Centering is not exclusive to a yoga class or a mystical meditation session. It means being "inwardly calm or steady." We were designed to experience this, yet it is elusive because we are bombarded with messages to make us feel less than so we do more. In my life as a parent, I have been called things like "super-woman, super-mom" or people have said "I don't know how you do all that you do," and I never really considered that a compliment. I don't want to be praised for seeming to be busy all the time. The truth is I wasn't as "busy" as most thought I was and I have learned to take time to rest. Think of being centered like the scale that the statue representing Lady Justice holds. It has two plates to hold whatever will be weighed out. Being centered is when everything feels level and balanced. Life will do its best to put plenty of things on the scale to throw off our balance. For each item it puts on us, we have to have a countermeasure that zeros out the effect.

A slippery slope to watch out for is the mantra of work crazy hard now so you can retire one day. This method has major flaws, but we validate it because it seems impressive. Again, our culture idolizes work. We have let our careers and our devotion to them define us. Missing out or "sacrificing" on very important life moments in the name of "one day" can impede and/or destroy relationships—especially that of a spouse or child. Relationships are built on experiences and moments together. Most will not have the patience to wait all the way to your retirement to resume. Be secure enough in who you are to enjoy life along the way. Fill it with things that breathe life into you like family table time, a hobby, hospitality and rest.

ENDNOTE:

1. Richard Exley. *The Rhythm of Life.* © 1987 Honor Books, Tulsa, Oklahoma. (p. 73.)

CHAPTER SEVEN

7

UNCOMMON CENTS

LEVEL PLAYING FIELD

Thomas Jefferson said it best: "We hold these truths to be self-evident: that all men are created equal; that they are endowed by their Creator with certain unalienable rights; that among these are life, liberty, and the pursuit of happiness." What did he mean by equality? This is the "less-than-self-evident" truth. Male is not equal to female, rich is not equal to poor, tall is not equal to short, beautiful is not equal to "bless your heart," you see where I am going. But, we are all equal in the number of hours we have in a day. Time is the great equalizer.

No matter how smart, how rich, or how successful we are, we are still subject to time. It is our truest form of currency. It is what we trade for money when we show up to work. We expect that if we do a certain job we will receive an agreed upon compensation. We have all heard the expression "time is money," but time is simply time. We trade it for money. The higher our skill level, training, education, talent, and experience take us, the higher our trade value can become. Should one neglect to improve themselves on some level, the rate of income will remain stagnant while the price of goods goes up.

RATE OF EXCHANGE

Most of us have no idea what our actual hourly wage is. We know how much the paycheck is, but have we ever stopped to calculate how much income there actually is after we factor in the expense of working? To find out your actual hourly wage (should you be so brave), start with what you make per month AFTER all deductions for taxes, insurance, 401k, and other deductible "benefits" have been removed. Be sure to divide that number by actual hours worked. Then add up the financial expenses of working like childcare, dry-cleaning, transportation (prorated amounts for gas, insurance, wear and tear), time spent commuting, office gifts, work clothes, personal maintenance for work, any lunch meals eaten out, travel costs (including hours away from home). Add the additional time to the hours worked and subtract the work related costs from your net income. Divide the remaining income by the total number of hours and voila! Now, don't cry. This is not meant to make you feel bad or inferior or anything like that. It is an exercise to help you see what the actual take home rate of exchange is for one hour of your life at work. This is the money that you get to decide where it goes after it is deposited into your bank account. This information really is powerful if you let it sink in. One of my personal favorite authors on the topic of money has to be Dave Ramsey. I will give you several of my all-time favorite quotes of his in this chapter. He and his wife Sharon have lived by their motto, "If you live like no one else, you can live like no one else."

Two months after we were married, Ted and I began Ramsey's Financial Peace University in Nashville, Tennessee. We wanted to start our marriage off on the best footing possible and since most divorces result from a financial issue we thought it best to get on the same page fast. We graduated and learned many invaluable truths that are a part of the fabric of our marriage to this day. One of the key things for me was the part about impulsive purchases and not knowing if you could afford something. Years later, when I began teaching a money class at our church, I had the thought of calculating what it really costs when we purchase something hence the true hourly wage exercise. Let's say you would like a new television for the family room. Your rationalization skills are peaking and you are ready to seal the deal. The one you want is around $695.00 and your mind instantly goes to work thinking of your bank account and how this new toy could make its way to your home. Yes, you may have enough money in the bank to pay for it, but what does it cost you? If your gross pay is $20/hr, you are looking at 34.75 hours of work for that television. BUT if you measure it by your true hourly wage of $11.30/hr, it really is 61.5 hours. That is perspective. That is information which may (or may not) change your mind on the television. It is important to know what your rate of exchange is and how you will use it to stay connected to your values.

I WANT AN OOMPA LOOMPA!

One of my favorite movies growing up was the original Willy Wonka and the Chocolate Factory. I imagined I was one of the children who found a golden ticket and was going through each and every room in the "world of pure imagination." Each time I watched the show, I would identify with one particular child character, but I would say what I would have done differently. The one I never liked was Veruca Salt. She had no redeeming qualities. She was a spoiled brat with a demanding personality. She had no patience or personal work ethic. She wanted everything handed to her instantaneously. As much as we all would like to think that the "I want it NOW" mentality is exclusive to Veruca, it is actually a poignant portrayal of the inner child we all struggle with when it comes to how we handle our finances. V.S.S. or Veruca Salt Syndrome has many symptoms. One of the most recognizable symptoms is the buy it before you can afford it behavior. Whether it's a car, vacation, jewelry, phone or entertainment, it bears the mark of V.S.S. if it comes before meeting the demands of the necessities.

We each have an inner child that loves to rant and kick and yell, but must learn to wait their turn. Money is like fuel. Any money earned must first take us where we need to go. Then after that, you have options. It is important to know that if you are already in a position where your money goes further than your bills, the remainder doesn't all feed the beast inside. Some needs to be set aside for the future and to give to worthy causes.

If we were to look right now, what would your bank records indicate that you value? Where we find the money trail we can find the heart right behind it.

- Do you value having a safety net in place for you and your family?

- Have you set your family up with a plan?

- Do you spend money like there is no tomorrow?

- Do you keep up with the Joneses at the cost of financial security?

- Are you tight-fisted with money, thus damaging close relationships with those in your household?

- Do you value giving to those causes who could never repay?

The point of all of these questions is to examine the behavior to see what you value. None of these questions has anything to do with how much money you have or don't have. Most of us aren't born into wealth; we have had very small beginnings. For many, their identity is found in how much they make, what kind of lifestyle they can provide for themselves and their family, the kind of car they drive, the trips they take, and the support staff they can afford to hire. Again, each of those "things" aren't bad things, they simply define what the person values. There are times when a want is worthy. I see the value in buying brands or products that have solid reputations for performance, longevity, and functionality. I don't like spending money that Ted or I worked very hard for on something less expensive that will likely breakdown before it should or lose its usefulness because it didn't have all we would eventually need out of it. We usually agree that it is worth the wait for the greater investment to get the better quality item than getting a cheaper one sooner. We do our best to make no purchases rooted in the need for approval or envy. Those purchases tend to be a burden anyways. We need a lot less than we actually think we do and so do our children. I am reminded of the story of when Ted's parents brought him home from the hospital all those years ago. His dad was around twenty and his mom was sixteen. They didn't have much, but they had their little family. They didn't have a crib so they used a dresser drawer as one. Most of us couldn't fathom putting a baby in a drawer, but I can assure you, he turned out just fine. The key is to get wise. "The beginning of wisdom is this: Get wisdom. Though it cost you all you have get understanding" (Proverbs 4:7). I would encourage you to pick up several great resources on money like, *Total Money Makeover* by Dave Ramsey and *Rich Dad, Poor Dad* by Robert Kiyosaki to get started. Financial wisdom is a value worth gaining and living out. It knows no limits and has the power to let you live more of your values and even beyond yourself.

POWER OF AGREEMENT

If you are married or share finances with someone else, it is important that you both be on the same page financially. One of my favorite quotes from Dave Ramsey's live event in Nashville was, "When you agree upon your budget, you agree upon your dreams." I know the word budget has a stigma to some, so I like to call it a spending map. When you gain agreement on how you will handle your money on a monthly basis, the goals you have that are a few years away will be met because you made those daily and monthly decisions to honor the values you have for your future. It is important to dream about your future. "If you aim at nothing, you will hit it every time." I know that I like to take a vacation every couple of years that involves sand and sun. I also know that I value not stressing about money while I am on said vacation. I like knowing that everything is paid for before I go which is why I prefer all-inclusive locations.

For our tenth wedding anniversary, I wanted to do something special. We have an arrangement where I plan even numbered anniversaries and he plans odds, so the tenth was my first big one to plan. We also have an arrangement that we get an allowance or personal "blow money" each month, and whatever we plan for gifts or trips comes from this slush fund. I began saving right after our eighth anniversary. Everything I got from our monthly personal money went straight into saving for this trip. It did take me two years to save, but we probably had the best week of our married life up to that point because we could enjoy every part of our vacation knowing there would be no surprise fees or accumulated expenses. Had I decided a couple of months before our anniversary to take the very same trip, it would have ended up being something we put on a credit card and then paid more for the trip than had we saved due to interest charges. I value getting the most bang for my buck so I plan ahead.

Money will flow where it is managed. If you are the manager of your money, then it will flow where you tell it. If you don't have a plan for your money, someone else does. Visa, Mastercard, and all the rest have a well thought out plan for your money. They tell you what they want you to do with their help all the time. Phrases like "you deserve" or "why wait" fuel V.S.S. and we begin to believe it if we allow those messages to distance us from our financial values. It is really important to define your financial values because so many aspects of life are legislated by money. Financial stress or strain is bad for your health. Losing sleep, stomach ulcers, blood pressure problems ... even suicidal thoughts are baggage that financial stress can bring to our health. Marriages suffer as well as a result of financial problems. Broken trust, arguing, loss of respect, and anger can be difficult to come back from for some couples.

WHAT WILL THEY REMEMBER?

Money itself is a magnifier of the heart. The reason money has the power it does is that is always displays motivation. After time, money is the second most powerful revealer of one's values. This is especially important when it comes to our children. We think a room full of toys, a schedule full of activities, and a closet full of clothes will fulfill their needs when in reality it doesn't. What do you remember from when you were around eight years old? Can you remember each toy, every outfit, all the sports gear? NO! Well, at least I can't. I can only remember a few actual things that were special, but I cherish all the memories I had with my family. My parents traveled a lot when I was a school-aged kid. My mom would instinctively buy us something while she was gone to somehow make up for the time. I can't tell you what those things were because at the end

> **Money is a magnifier of the heart—it displays your motivation**

of the day, they didn't matter. I remember the times they were home. My dad sometimes would blow dry my hair with a "curly brush" otherwise known as a round brush and it made my hair silky and beautiful. I love that memory. I remember my mom writing me notes and letters nearly every day I was away for college. Sometimes she would just kiss the inside of a card with her bright pink lipstick. I loved all of those. With children, quality will win over quantity every time. They don't need more stuff or more activities; they need more of you. If you have set yourself up financially that working more hours for more days must be done, then reassess where your values lie with regards to money and spending. You may see that you are making choices that don't end up having the positive effect you thought they would.

CAUGHT, NOT TAUGHT

Being present in your children's lives allows you the privilege of modeling your values. Your children will pick up more from what they see you do than what they hear you say, hence the phrase, "caught, not taught." I can say to my four, "You should really care for the hungry kids in our community," until I am blue in the face and they may never do one thing about it. However, if I take them to our church when it is time to pack the weekend food bags for the local school kids who are food insecure and pack food bags with them, they will see my heart is in it too. I can tell them, "You need to respect your daddy," but if I don't demonstrate respect with my words or actions, they will not. I can tell them I love them, but if I don't show it in a way they understand or receive love, then it doesn't translate. My son Luke loves all things boy like sports, cars, fishing, army men, and warrior gear. If I told him, "I show you I love you by working hard all day for our family," he won't understand what love really means with his current level of mental development. How he picks up on love is by me engaging him in what he likes to do or snuggling up on the couch watching a movie he wants to see. I don't want to see him develop into a man whose only view of loving his kids is working harder. We can't assume that children possess the cognitive power to understand all we do for them and how it translates as love in our minds.

One of the most powerful things I have had the blessing to observe is my mother's generous heart. She is one of the most thoughtful people I know and it is something she uses to bless not only her children, but so many she comes into contact with. When she was a child, her mother was a single mom of two. They didn't have a lot and she knew what it was like to watch her mom get items out of grocery store dumpsters to provide food at times. When the man whom I know as my Poppa married my Grandma, he rescued them all which set up our family later for a much better life in many ways.

My Poppa was one of the most generous men I have ever known. Any time my Grandma told of the days where they didn't have enough food, his eyes would well up with tears and you could see him wish he could have been there to do something about it. He was a retired CPA and had always been very responsible with his money. As I got older, they were very helpful when certain expenses would arise. They would bless my sisters and me and it would always be at the perfect time. My mother models the value of generosity still to this day. Between my mom and my grandparents, there is a huge legacy of being a financial blessing.

There are many things in my life today I would not have if it had not been for their generosity. My parents did their very best to provide us the best education. It is something that can never be taken away from us and we are all better for it. It came at a huge cost. They sacrificed much ... almost too much ... to keep us in the schools we attended. I do not ever take for granted what that cost them, and I realize this was an expression of genuine love.

When you examine your values in the area of money, consider the area of generosity. The legacy that it can bring to your family and your future family will have a compounded effect. This is not the give-them-everything-they-want kind of generosity, but rather the ability to launch them further than they could get on their own. "The world of the generous gets larger and larger, the world of the stingy gets smaller and smaller" (Proverbs 11:24).

The legacy I will leave for my children will be one of stewardship facilitating generosity. What that wordy phrase simply means to me is taking good care of the dollars and cents so I can give them away when I feel the impetus to. To do this I must avoid paying more for things than I have to. This requires staying out of debt as much as possible, being content with certain things longer than I would like, shopping around to find the best prices, saying "not now" to some things or finding ways to save on them and working smarter using what now has become uncommon sense financially.

Because generosity is high in my value order, I am careful how and where I spend my dollars and cents

THINGS ARE NOT ALWAYS AS THEY SEEM

It is imperative to wrap your brain around the fact that there may not be a certain look to living out your financial values like you once thought. Think about how you know if someone is successful with their health. What would you see? They would likely be lean, strong, and eat clean, etc. You can see it though. It is a visible value. What about the person who is successful in their education and brain power. How could you tell if they were devoted to a high value on education? You could hear them speak or watch them demonstrate their knowledge and know they are smart. It is a visible value.

Things get tricky with money. Financial success is not easily measured by appearances. Many times people who have a lot of nice things are not financially successful, they are simply good at acquiring debt. Most millionaires don't live like they have the money they do. This is what keeps them millionaires. Legacy is not found in possessions or the amount of toys one has when they die. It is found in how far beyond yourself you thought and how that determined what you did with the money you made.

Chapter Eight

8

THE FAITH FILTER

• •

This is probably the chapter I am most excited about because faith is where so much of our individuality is able to reveal itself. Faith allows us to try things that make little to no sense to our minds. Imagination is useless without attaching any faith to it. A fitting example would be the Wright Brothers, Orville and Wilbur. Their curiosity, intellectual prowess, and belief in the possibility of something being done that had never been done before materialized with the first successful flight in 1903. I also think about the early doctors having the faith to move an organ from one individual to another in hopes of saving a life. So many noble and heroic achievements have occurred because people dared to believe and act on that belief.

FIRM FOUNDATIONS

For my family, faith has remained a constant despite tragedy or perceived setbacks. This doesn't mean that we pretended we were fine or unmoved by events, but that we knew once we calmed down that God was for us and He would carry us through. There have been times when we felt the winds of change come and point us in a direction that required a great deal of faith. In 2012, Ted's father came to live with us in Nashville, and in 2013 we added baby #4 to the mix. Our house was getting a little crowded so we began looking for other options in our area and price range. The hunt was rather difficult so we started to call our mystery house a "unicorn" because it was very hard to find. Nothing was panning out. We went so far as to have an architect and builder come to our current home to see if we could add on. It was looking like a possibility but something bugged me.

When I would ask, "Should we add on to this house, making it one of the largest homes in our subdivision?" everyone had the same response. They all said, "No, unless this is your forever home." Well how was I to know what I would be doing forever? It seemed senseless to risk all of that money on something I wasn't sure of, so we began saving money that would either go toward our expansion or to the purchase of our unicorn. In July of 2014, we were just one semester away from Ted finishing up his Bachelor's degree and things were really coming to a head as far as needing to decide where we were going to live. He and I were asked to speak at a relationships conference in the Houston area and we felt led to give a financial gift to the ministry that had us out. We told them this was a seed for our house. We desperately wanted to know where we were to settle and we prayed that God would speak to our hearts quickly. That was a Saturday.

The following Monday night, Ted and I were having an important discussion in the parking lot of Bed, Bath and Beyond, where all important conversations happen, and we felt God speak to our hearts that we were to move to back to Texas. This was not a move either of us could have foreseen or would have really been expecting at all since my business was doing really well and he had several relationships with the local hospitals that would easily lead to a job. This was completely out of our box.

This is where our foundation of faith kicked in. This move wasn't just about being closer to our family, even though that was a benefit. It wasn't about moving back to the greatest state in America, even thought that was also a benefit. It was about positioning our family for our next level of living and new direction. This had nothing to do with money but everything to do with authentic purpose and living our values.

> **Moving in response to our authentic purpose and living our values required faith**

This book was one of the things that came from the move. My schedule in Nashville between work, homeschooling, and other activities, didn't lend itself to multiple hour blocks to pour my heart out on paper. We knew that we could trust where we were being led. God doesn't set us up for failure; He sets us up to engage our faith and grow. For most of my life I hadn't really wanted to be a person of large influence. I knew I could help people around me through small groups and a few seminars, but to put myself out there was another thing. I didn't want to be subject to public opinion or criticism. That vulnerability was a result of a lack of identity on my part. Now that I know more of what I value and why, there is a faith-filled freedom to be who I was created to be and help who I was designed to help.

DIVINELY DESIGNED

You and I were not just an idea of our parents. We were an intentional idea by our Creator. A man at our church reminded me recently that, "The same God who said, 'Let there be light' said 'Let there be you!'" This really hit home with me. God designed us with things in common with one another, but the things that make us unique are in the details. Fingerprints, DNA, vocal tone, retinas, personality, and what we value. Think of all the security measures you have even seen in real life or on a movie screen. They are all things to ensure that only authorized persons gain access. The same is true for us and our values. Our unique make-up opens doors only meant for us. We must be willing to be true to ourselves and remain in our lanes to access our destinies and reach all we were made to reach.

The great thing about the way we were created is that there is no waste. In fact we were not divinely designed with the limited capacity to only care for and provide for ourselves. We were made to do more, to be more than we ever would need on our own.

GREATNESS LEADS TO GENEROSITY

We are each a part of a greater whole—an important part, but just a piece, not the whole deal. When you realize this and begin living for things greater than yourself, your influence begins to expand and increase. When this influence is used for good, many lives can be changed for the better. Have you thought about anyone's needs outside of your own in a while? Is there a people group that you notice being neglected or suffering some disservice? You have the eyes for them because you are a part of the solution for them. Again, we are each unique. We are each a solution to a different problem, which is why it is imperative we be ourselves. Without that, we would miss something or someone.

Once you identify your cause, get behind it. Invest and be a part of real change for it. This not only benefits the ones you are helping, it also radiates to you and your family. There are not many family activities I enjoy more than service opportunities. We trade an afternoon piddling around at home for an afternoon of purpose. We take each opportunity to tell our children why we are doing it and why their help matters. We do our best to put a face with a cause. Like with the food bag packing, I remind them that there are children who don't have a pantry or refrigerator full of food to choose from when they get home. Some of them don't have parents even present so they must fend for themselves. Every can of food or box of cereal you pack makes a difference in their lives. They don't go home afraid of being hungry for the weekend. They can relax knowing that there is at least what we are supplying them with to eat. They will then do better in school and hopefully graduate and find a career. It is so great to rally around such a worthy cause with a portion of our time together as a family.

THE THREE T'S

Faith allows us to see that what we are doing for others matters on a much larger scale. When we view all of our actions through the lens of faith, we can see the thread that connects us to one another with great clarity. These connections are made when we give of ourselves via our three t's:

- Time
- Talent
- Treasure

We leave a piece of ourselves behind like a seed in the soil of someone else's life and let it grow. Yes, these things cost us. They may force us to rearrange our schedule. But they are worthy of the cost and we will be better because of them. God brilliantly created a beneficial response in our bodies when we do good things. Scientists call it the "helper's high." In a WebMD archive called, "The Science of Good Deeds," the author discusses some of the findings in several of their investigative studies. "Two large studies found that older adults who volunteered reaped benefits in their health and well-being. Those who volunteered were living longer than non-volunteers. Another large study found a 44% reduction in early death among those who volunteered a lot—a greater effect than exercising four times a week." For those of you who hate to exercise, you may have found your winner here!

How fantastic that none of our actions are wasted. Nothing we do for others leaves us worse off than before we did it. Scientists may never understand all the physical benefits and that's okay to me. I don't need them to be able to articulate for me why I feel so good after helping a person or people who could never return the favor. I know it, because I feel it, and it feels great.

CONVICTION REQUIRES ACTION

Thomas Carlyle once said, "Conviction is worthless unless it is converted into conduct." It doesn't matter what we believe if we never attach any action to it. We are only a notable force once there is something we have invested into something we believe. Demonstrating your convictions is the first step in leadership. If you see an injustice that is within your power to correct, it demands action. Faith is the cohesive ingredient that binds our beliefs to our actions.

Faith is what separates the ordinary from the extraordinary. Faith negates fear. Faith says, "It can be done, and it is worth doing." If there are values you have discovered you have but are not yet being acted upon, faith is the platform from which you can correct your course. There are worthwhile things in life that are difficult to tackle with plenty of reason to use caution when considering the cost and benefits. One of these for our family was the idea of Ted getting a Bachelor's Degree in Nursing. He mentioned the idea

> *Faith is the platform from which you can correct your course*

when we first were married but we both dismissed it because he was the one with the job and the insurance and I was in the middle of a business upstart making little to no money. Around eight years later, the topic came up again. He was stuck in a warehouse job getting passed over for every promotion (to the one management spot at his branch). The benefits were good and the vacation time was plentiful, but he was feeling no fulfillment and coming home overly exhausted every day.

The lack of purpose he felt in his job got to such a high level it made a change absolutely necessary. My business by this time was doing well enough that I could cover the expenses except for private insurance. We would need a solution for this because we had three little ones with one of them being a newborn. He asked his employer if they would work with his nursing school schedule and they agreed, so we bought books and signed up and paid for classes. We were all set as far as a plan but the plan looked very rough. Ted would work 40+ hours a week, be a full-time nursing student, study and sleep in the remaining hours. I knew this was not going to be a picnic. In fact, I grieved and cried knowing what an uphill journey this was going to be. I would basically be a single working mom and he would be eternally busy and tired. Yes, the goal of him being a nurse was worth beginning, but we prayed for a better solution to the insurance portion. Not many days after he was all registered, his employer told him they had to change their mind and revoked his flexible schedule. This was a move to force Ted out as he was one of the higher paid staff since he had worked there so long. It was devastating at the time, but one of the best things that could have happened. Faith said, "Begin"—even without every single detail explained. We prayed for a solution that in my mom's words would be the "best of both," meaning he would get insurance but not have to work all those hours. We took out a major medical policy to bridge us to something and watched for it all to be worked out. By the first week of December, Ted had an amazing part-time job with full benefits, vacation, and even paid paternity leave! We had never seen a company with that and he was able to work for them even through our move to Texas where he began his nursing career following graduation. God is faithful!

One thing you have to know for yourself is where your heart is leading you. There were several voices telling us to stay where it was safe. Fear prevents fulfillment. Fear hinders you from stepping into your destiny by causing you to never try. Yes, sometimes failure is a possibility, but so is success. Before we began the journey of Ted's college years, I knew what it would cost us. I knew for that season, quality time together would be less and demands would be higher. His first year of college was probably the hardest year of my life. On this side of it, I am thankful I stayed the course. Faith said, "Persevere." Faith said to keep my eyes on the promise, endure the necessary challenges and it would all be worth it. Faith reminds you of your end goal. Faith keeps your focus on the finish line, not on the obstacles between you and breaking the tape.

Faith allows you to keep your eyes on the promise and endure necessary challenges

During the four and a half year process, there were plenty of times we had to remind ourselves that we loved each other, that we were still each other's favorites, and each day we endured we were closer to its completion. I am a countdown girl. If something important is coming up, there is a good chance I have a countdown meter going so I can see just how far away it is. It keeps me connected to the end, the goal, the result that all this effort is for. It is worth enduring the things we don't enjoy so much so we can get to the things we enjoy very much. Endurance is an act of faith. Champions. Endure.

Even though Ted was in school and it was a crazy season of life, we knew we wanted a fourth child. Gluttons for punishment? Maybe, but we really loved our children and thought a fourth would round us out. I was thrilled when I could give my mom the card letting her know she had another grand coming. I had the perfect plan: I would be done having all of my children by thirty-five. My sister also found out she was expecting and our due dates were just three days apart. It was fantastic! We went to our first ultrasound and saw the little blip on the screen and something didn't feel right. We had been here before and by this many weeks, that little blip should have been bigger. The heartbeat was about 100 beats per minute, which was low. Our doctor told us that we needed to come back in two weeks to check for growth. Two weeks later we found out that our little one had passed and we had miscarried. I was shocked. I can't describe the hurt. We were broken, with a sadness like I had never experienced before

We grieved the loss of our little one for several months, especially when we would find out other friends of ours were expecting. I didn't know if I could bear to go through anything like that again. Faith said, "You can." Faith said, "This is not how your story ends." It would have been easy just to stop trying following a disaster like that. We had three healthy kids, why risk screwing that up? God knew my heart was for another baby, but I needed the courage to believe He would fulfill my heart's desire, I needed faith.

A few months later we made a "tenth anniversary vacation special" ... adding the fourth arrow in our quiver, right in the middle of Ted's educational pursuit. The blessing of twelve weeks paid leave took us through the end of that semester, and then summer break gave us some very special time together as a family. God knew that our best plan could not and would not compare to what He had for us. No matter how hard we work to try to make something happen, it can never compare to what doors open with one touch of faith.

Faith is actually a response of trust. It comes once you have reached the end of what you know or what you can see and helps you take the next step. It grows the more it is utilized. It is so beautiful that you can give your faith to someone who doesn't have any of their own and it will multiply. Many times my mom encouraged me to write a book, but I didn't feel like I had anything worth sharing. I had to borrow from her faith to even begin. The more time I spent writing, the stronger my own faith became. I realized by writing that even if I helped no one else, I have helped myself. Even greater, I left a view of my heart for my children to always have. Faith doesn't run from things just because they are difficult. Faith is the first to step into the battle. Faith is a muscle—ready and able to become stronger with every challenge.

The truth is that all of our values are filtered by faith. What makes the difference is the quality and strength of the filter.

Some filters are not strong enough or dense enough to keep out toxic thoughts, causing us to be self-defeated before we even begin. The people who we see breaking records, improving technology, curing diseases, and fighting for change all first believe it is possible. This doesn't mean they never run across feelings of doubt or discouragement. It simply means they push through them.

I love watching the Olympics when a world record is broken or they have added another rotation to an ice skating jump, believed impossible for anyone to achieve. By one athlete breaking the barrier, by the next competition, no athlete will even make it to the final round if they can't match the performance. Faith is like that. When exercised, it opens doors for others, not just you!

Filtering out what is contrary to your goal or a barrier to you taking your next step will fuel you. Ask yourself these questions:

- Are those speaking doubt over you speaking from their own failures or limitations?
- Did someone they know try something similar but not complete it, or complete it without success?
- Do they feel bad because your courage outs their cowardice?
- Are their best days long in the past?
- Do they feel that something about you should disqualify you?

Separate yourself from these voices. Love them from a distance if you must, but keep what your faith has for you to do in your crosshairs. If you see someone else on a similar path as you, encourage them. You know firsthand the struggle. Communicate with them the things that help you get through. Success is lonely if you help no one else get there. Focus, follow through, and finish. Nothing feels as good as reaching your goals and dreams surrounded by those whom you have loved and encouraged along the way.

Faith is the response of trust, allowing you to go beyond what you can see or know

Chapter Nine

9

CONCLUSION

If you value being trustworthy, model honesty and drop the gossip. If you value time with your family, survey how you spend your time and edit out the things that are of lower value or reduce the amount of time you spend on those things. If you value personal growth—spiritually, educationally, experientially—make room in your life to invest in this growth. Realize this will come at the expense of something else you are doing, decide what things are important to you and make your calendar and your bank account support those decisions.

To step out into uncharted territory is simply a decision not to put another step where you are or have been before. I have the same number of hours in a day as my single friends who talk about how they hardly have time for anything. With four children, two dogs, a husband and a career, I still have time to fiddle with. I have time to allocate to causes I deem worthy and people I can invest in or be invested into by them. The time you have will ultimately be deposited into one category or another. The decision, for the most part, is yours. You are a managed-decision away from living the life you have in your head. The gaps between where you are and where you want to be begin to close the more you give way to who you are and how you were divinely designed to be.

KNOWING IS HALF THE BATTLE

Hopefully by this point in the book you have begun to articulate your values more closely and connect to them authentically. The good news is once you know them, you are half way there. But there is still more to do. Living your values requires that boldness and faith we talked about. It may require quite a bit of change and that hurts sometimes. It may require letting go of something good to get to something great. Don't be surprised if you feel resistance from those most familiar with you once you begin incorporating things that are in line with your values and excluding those things that aren't. Before you blast them with your values and reasons for changing, take a moment to understand where they are coming from. If you have always coached little league but decide that it no longer fits into your value system, it may come as a surprise to them. Nothing bad has to happen in order for change to occur.

Change can come from a dream in your heart you are ready to embrace with all the courage you can muster. When you change, it affects everyone under your influence, and that may be more people than you realize. Not everyone is ready for change just because you are. People like things to remain the same much more than they would be willing to admit. There is something great about going back to the places we grew up to find the restaurants with our favorite food still in operation, despite our not being there for a while.

We love memorabilia and enjoy nostalgic feelings, but they are not always the building blocks for our current value order. They are more like a really comfy chair that is hard to get motivated to get out of. Comfort can be your worst enemy. Sticking with something because, "why fix what's not broken," will stunt the growth you need for your next season in life. Imagine if a newborn had the choice to remain a baby or grow up. Yes, there are things that are quite comfortable about being completely taken care of and having no responsibilities, but after a while the limitations that go along with being a baby will grow old. We were created to mature.

As parents we appreciate the fact that most of our children grow to be independent. We agree to take care of them, serve them, provide for them, and protect them for a season of their lives, but there comes the time when their wings are ready for flight and they must launch. I don't know many parents who would say they would be willing to do all of those things for a perfectly capable adult child for the rest of its life. Changing diapers, cutting up tiny bits of bland food, and getting up in the middle of the night would be ridiculous for a twenty year old baby! Yet, many find themselves twenty years into a dream, still in its infancy, where not one step toward development of the dream has been taken. Growth without change is impossible.

If children are too comfortable at home, they tend to stay around longer than they should. Part of the job of the parent is to de-feather the nest. True love and commitment to a child's destiny requires that we love them enough to make life at home something they desire for the appropriate season, gradually changing into a desire to create a home of their own.

Life has a way of doing the same thing to us. Work becomes just miserable enough that we begin to think about other possibilities. Next thing you know, an opportunity presents itself and you make the leap. But if things never became uncomfortable, the change would never have manifested. If you find yourself in the throws of what may feel like transition coming, be on the lookout for something new to draw you out of your comfort zone and into an area of new growth. If you are on the heels of a disappointment or failure, take the time to learn from it, evaluate and adjust. Come back better and stronger.

Transition is often preceded by something difficult which draws us out of our comfort zone

My son and I love reading about Thomas Edison. He is one of my favorite people because of what he overcame in order to become who he was designed to be. His teachers in elementary school considered him a problem child, but his mother knew he had a gift. She pulled him from school and taught him at home. He worked selling newspapers on trains to support his laboratory expenses as a young boy. He didn't have any friends who were like him in his insistence on developing inventions with their spare time. He had this drive within himself and it placed a demand on his time. He is credited with numerous inventions and discoveries, but what is rarely talked about were the numerous failures or dead-ends he experienced along the way. It took his willingness to persevere and try new things to finally arrive at each new invention. It was from a series of failures, coupled with the courage to try again and the awareness to evaluate what went wrong that Edison found success. For many of us, it takes just one failed attempt to make us want to quit. The prevalence of low level resolve makes it really simple for those willing to try even one more time to succeed. As with most things, you can't win if you don't play. Be compelled to defy your fear of failure. The feeling at the finish line is worth it.

From our thought patterns, grooves or ruts develop in our mental "roads." Unless we begin to think differently, we will never be able to accomplish anything new. Who knows what you have yet to invent? Whose lives will be improved by something you thought of and had the courage to build? Life is more than feeling like you are on a hamster wheel working so hard but going nowhere. We look at that hamster and think, "If you would only step out to the side instead of going in the same direction you always have, you could get off that thing!" The same is true for those of us who feel stuck, like progress toward our values is nowhere to be seen. Sometimes it is as easy as doing one thing slightly different and seeing the change it brings.

When new things are begun, they don't usually start out fully developed. We would think it was crazy if someone said they were going to birth an adult, yet we think that dreams or goals should manifest faster than microwave pizza. Life is not only a journey, it is also a constant learning process … if you allow it.

There will be milestones you reach and celebrate along the way, and each of those milestones will have more meaning the greater their congruence with your value order.

THE SQUEEZE

When major seasons are changing, be aware that there will be intense pressure shifts. As you close the current chapter and begin to move forward into the next, some parts may come with unusual amounts of pain and grief. I experienced this personally when I decided to fully commit to share the message inside of me. For just over seven years, I was a "hair-apist"— a hairstylist, in layman's terms. In that amount of time, I had a very successful business that allowed me flexibility, creativity, and a comfortable income. Many of my clients were friends or became friends over time, so there was also a relational aspect of my work that was extremely fulfilling as well.

I taught classes and led numerous small groups through my church throughout the years and felt my passion for that growing, but didn't really want some of the challenges that come with doing that full-time. I was invited to speak at two conferences that had larger audiences than I was used to. The DNA I share with my grandmother who was an author and speaker, and my mother who is also an author and speaker, was surging to the surface after those events. I began to agree with God that my future included sharing my message and that He would give me the strength necessary to face the inherent challenges. The future looked great. I was so excited thinking and dreaming about what that would look like. But how do I leave what I have? How do I stop taking care of my friends, many of whom I would call "framily." These people have been with me through numerous children being born, Ted's schooling, life's ups and downs, how was I just going to stop and change directions?

There were several families I felt were on my radar more than others and I began to think, "Who will watch out for them?" I had the faith to take the leap for the new thing, but did I have the faith to end the thing I was in the middle of? How would I? This situation made me remember something my Grandma Frances told me when my music business wasn't doing well. She said, "Charity, never quit when it's bad. Don't quit while things are hard. If you are going to end something, end it while it is good." It kinda didn't make sense to me in the moment, because I thought when things were ugly would be the perfect time to be done. I felt like I was at the top of my game.

This made me think about all the sports folks who talk about retiring as their winning season is coming to a close. Then they go for one more season, often marked by underwhelming stats and a good injury or two. "Should have quit while you were ahead," was all I was thinking. That is how I had to choose to view my situation. There is a select window of time when we are able to make a graceful exit out of one thing and into another. You and I both know people who stayed too long in certain situations. The grace for them left and things didn't end as well as they could have. Timing was and is the key. Yes, finish strong and fulfill commitments, but when it is time to move on, move on.

> **Timing is everything—don't linger too long in a season that is trying to pass**

PERMISSION GRANTED

You have the freedom to follow your value order. You have all rights associated with being true to yourself and prioritizing your life in the way that you were created to. With all of that fun and fabulous freedom comes responsibility as well. You bear the weight of each and every choice you make. If certain things that took place in your past have skewed your value order and caused you to make poor choices, the perpetuation of those choices falls on you. The longer you continue the behavior or pattern that came from someone or something else hurting you or disappointing you, the more power you give it and the less value you give you. You will be stuck. The freedom that discovering and living your value order provides is the freedom to follow it, regardless of other people's values.

Another freedom that is almost equally as important is the freedom to not be critical or judgmental of other people's values. The more I embody my values and embrace the why's behind them, the more I realize how individual I am. These values are ones that I have carefully reasoned through. I have evaluated all the filters I was consciously using to arrive at them and I cannot make decisions based upon them with much more ease. Now the only time decisions are difficult is when there is a choice to be made that places two or more of my highly ranked values against each other. I do my best to find a third option and if there is not one, I simply take the scenarios and play out in all detail imaginable how they will affect me and my family. The best choice will always reveal itself in the details.

The more you can anticipate real results from your choices, the better choices you will make. This applies to so many things like selecting a mate, a job, a car, a vacation, your career track, your house, school ... even the way you commute to work. Too many times people are only able to see the pros or the cons in their situations. A person who only sees the pros tends to marry potential rather than reality, buy impulsively and short-sightedly, be late to things because they think there will be no traffic for them, and spend more than they should because they assume tomorrow will bring more than enough money to cover it. In contrast, the person who sees only the cons tends to be skeptical and critical of every possible mate, hence putting off or even never marrying, takes forever to make major purchases because, "What if they lose their job tomorrow?" They never get on the dance floor in order to completely prevent their toes from being stepped on, and rather than try anything new themselves, they watch and wait for those around them to fail when trying something new.

Yes, these are extreme generalizations, but you can see how crippling being unrealistic can be. I can recall times in my life where I could easily identify with both sides of this. Most of us as children were overly optimistic. We thought everything we ever wanted was easily attainable, that friends could play whenever we wanted to, a fish was waiting for us to cast our line into the water, and mom always would have gum in her purse. We didn't learn pessimism until we were older and realized those things weren't always the case and in fact, we may not ever get some of the things we always wanted.

The beauty of life is found in understanding our part in determining what we get out of it. The pain of living in conflict with your value order is undeniable and costly. Championing your alignment with your value order can be costly as well, but there is not the pain factor involved. There is energy, synergy, and momentum. You can feel this energy when you get around someone who is true to themselves and happy about it. They radiate. They are not insecure. They welcome your point of view in discussions and don't feel the need to convince you of theirs. They are comfortable in their own skin and aware both of their strengths and weaknesses. They don't bully. In fact, one of my hopes with this book is to help rehab the adult bully. I was one at different times in my life, my sisters can attest to that. I had segments of terrible insecurity, career frustration, moral compromise, and a legalistic no-tolerance attitude to boot. One thing for which I am most proud of myself is gaining confidence in me, myself, and why. I am forever grateful for those who have loved me through those phases and have let me become better. I am thankful for those who sharpened me and held me to a higher standard. I am even thankful for those who bullied me because they gave me eyes to see others being bullied and a heart to help them.

> **The pain of living in conflict with your value order is undeniable and costly**

LESS TALKING, MORE DOING

Here is your call to action.

- **First, discover your value order.** If by this point in the book you are still unsure of your value order, take the time over the next couple of days and begin writing down parts of your life that are important to you on note cards. Move them around until you get to an order that feels good. Remember your value order is flexible, especially as major life changes occur.

- **Second, evaluate your current position in relationship to your value order.** To find areas that conflict, think about things you hate doing or that require a ton of energy while leaving you drained. To find areas that flow with your value order, think about what you look forward to doing and things that fulfill you leaving you energized even though you may have exerted yourself.

- **Third, begin to make choices that bring you closer to your value order.** Even the smallest amount of progress will bring momentum, satisfaction, and a measure of joy. Once you start this portion of the process, you will feel yourself taking ownership for more and more decisions. You will find yourself making quality edits which will reinforce the things you do keep in your life.

- **Fourth, protect your value order.** As soon as you start solidifying your order, there will be things that come and test your commitment to it. People who are not as secure in who they are themselves will be the first to give you chances to abandon your resolve. Beware of good causes. They are powerful because they tug on our heart strings as they should. But it is possible to over-commit, making the quality of your contributions go down. Measure them up against your total order and make sure they are in line. Remember time is your currency. When you do finally reach your current best scenario, invest fully. Be present and engaged. Suck the marrow out of each moment as you will never have that moment back again. Celebrate the ones you love.

There is a good chance that people—family and close friends—are at or near the top of your value order. Take each opportunity you can to let them know you love them and appreciate them. Seasons change so rapidly that it can be hard to recall the minutia of the daily grind. However, with the quality of life you can give from, the impact you leave behind in the lives of others will be unforgettable. You were made a one of a kind and designed to live an original life. There are people you will have a lot of parallels with, people you will share certain mindsets with, but there are still things that are unique to you and your fingerprint you will leave behind. Embrace your unique design and let it propel you into your destiny.

MEET THE AUTHOR
CHARITY BRADSHAW

• •

As a mother of four children and dedicated wife of over twelve years, Charity Bradshaw has learned the power behind establishing your personal value system. She and her husband, Ted, are committed to living a life of excellent stewardship. Being a third generation author and speaker, Charity is a modern voice of hope and stability in today's rough waters. Pulling from practical life experiences and using down-to-earth humor, many have been impacted by the relevant truth she releases.

By sharing her message on the power of values as "beacons" for our lives, she has developed a time-tested approach applicable to individuals, small church groups, and corporations. She offers real life keys to honoring and cultivating those established values which allows for immediate actionable steps that yield positive growth results in your personal life.

Charity's heart is that everyday people would be transformed through her passionate teaching. From your own backyard to the workplace to the world, Charity believes that every life touched will bring light to those around them.

For more information, to connect,
or to invite Charity to speak at your event, visit:

WWW.CHARITYBRADSHAW.COM